What You See
When You Can't See

What You See When You Can't See

How Blindness Helped One Woman
Discover the True Beauty of Life

ZENA COOPER

HAY HOUSE

Carlsbad, California • New York City
London • Sydney • New Delhi

Published in the United Kingdom by:
Hay House UK Ltd, The Sixth Floor, Watson House,
54 Baker Street, London W1U 7BU
Tel: +44 (0)20 3927 7290; Fax: +44 (0)20 3927 7291
www.hayhouse.co.uk

Published in the United States of America by:
Hay House Inc., PO Box 5100, Carlsbad, CA 92018-5100
Tel: (1) 760 431 7695 or (800) 654 5126
Fax: (1) 760 431 6948 or (800) 650 5115; www.hayhouse.com

Published in Australia by:
Hay House Australia Ltd, 18/36 Ralph St, Alexandria NSW 2015
Tel: (61) 2 9669 4299; Fax: (61) 2 9669 4144; www.hayhouse.com.au

Published in India by:
Hay House Publishers India, Muskaan Complex,
Plot No.3, B-2, Vasant Kunj, New Delhi 110 070
Tel: (91) 11 4176 1620; Fax: (91) 11 4176 1630; www.hayhouse.co.in

A catalogue record for this book is available from the British Library.

Tradepaper ISBN: 978-1-78817-319-3
Audiobook ISBN: 978-1-78817-371-1
E-book ISBN: 978-1-78817-326-1

Printed and bound by CPI Group (UK) Ltd, Croydon, CR0 4YY

Contents

CHAPTER 1

The Beauty in Blindness

'The poor, poor souls. What is it they see? What would it be like to see the world through their eyes? It must be awful to have vision like that. I just can't imagine what it's like for them to live with the sight (or lack of) that they have. They must miss out so much on the true meaning of life. Bless them. After all, who would want to see with perfect vision, as they're so busy looking with their eyes, they have forgotten to look with their heart.'

With three white cursors flashing on the dark screen, I focus in on what I think is the middle one. As each cursor merges with the next in a captivating haze, my mind starts to play 'Give us a clue'. With four large, wobbly words typed on my magnified screen, my fingers trace the keyboard for the right keys to tap away at next. I really want to stop annoying the narrator on my computer, as although she patiently alerts me to yet another mistake I've made, I'm sure I can hear her impatience grow. Is that possible? As I can only see a triple-vision blurry mass in front of me, my eyes try to decipher what my fingers have typed. It looks about the size of a six-letter word that takes up the whole screen. The first letter is larger and rounded at the top, so I guess it's a 'b'. The last letter drops down below the others, so I guess that's the 'y'. By this method of deduction, my brain tells me I've typed in the word 'beauty' correctly. In an almost surprised voice, the usually narky narrator confirms it, and I feel elated: this time-consuming process is finally getting me somewhere.

Typing while blind is not the easiest of tasks, but when I get it right it's the most fulfilling feeling ever. Even if it does take what feels like an eternity to do what most people do in seconds, it's still done.

In many ways, I feel like the outsider looking in on a world full of people who don't always appreciate the gifts they receive each day. The gift of being able to read words from afar has always left me speechless: when a person reads words on a sign from many feet away without needing binoculars, it feels like I'm standing next to a superhero. How people recognize others down a street without having to hear their voices is another unsolved mystery. Do they know something I don't?

For the sighted, sightseeing must be a tick-list haven rather than a health and safety nightmare. I've heard rumours that in the sighted world they use those superhero eyes to live in an altered state, using only their vision to live day by day. What must that be like? And yet, in other ways, it feels like I live inside the world of truth, observing many people living a half-hearted life full of voids. Seeing people not living their lives fully can be frustrating.

Blindness affects individuals differently. There's no universal answer to 'What is it like to be blind?', yet to me, blindness is the key connection to the true meaning of life. Growing up with impaired vision that I hid from the outside world meant I learned to live in an alternative way. I learned to be self-reliant from a young age. I learned that people and situations can be transient, yet nature is a constant. I learned that others used their vision to tell them about the outside world, while I used my intuition and other senses. I learned that the world was bigger than any problem that presented itself. I also learned that people's poor decisions don't define who they really are. A part of me would love to call the unsighted world the world of insights; living without functional vision really does give you insight into the real meaning of life.

The bridge between the sighted and unsighted world can be rickety. Many people may go from being sighted to losing their sight, remaining permanently on the sight-loss side of the bridge; only a few cross into the visual world after surgery. Yet, on whichever side of the bridge we dwell, I know there's a whole world surrounding us, and it's full of happiness should we choose to embrace it.

I've lived my life in the unsighted world, but for four months I lived in the middle of that bridge. After surgery in my right eye I gained a little more sight – it was not functional vision, but for the first time ever I was able to make out faces; I could see the ophthalmologist and my partner. Close up, I could see the shape of their eyes, their nostrils and the outlines of their mouths. I then found I could kind of read the sign on the front of the bus (although it was still more guesswork than precision). I remember thinking, *This is a taste of what it must be like to see.* It was not easy to get used to, as the contrast between the two eyes was immense. Seeing with my right eye was like looking through a warped telescope rather than a blurry veil. I was in a hall of mirrors in a sensory-filled fairground where ants appear two feet tall and sticks look like tree trunks. Confusion was an understatement, but at least the experience gave me a little clarity around what it was like to live with sight. Later, I discovered that the surgery had caused irreversible damage. And this meant that I now had reduced vision in an already blurry world. I underwent another operation to remove my lens implant, which meant reverting to my old way of life. As mad as this may sound, my reduced vision meant sinking into a more blissful existence.

After dipping a toe into the sighted world, I was glad to return to the safe world I'd grown up in. Living without much sight in a sighted world felt like I was an undercover detective casing the place for clues on how the sighted lived. I figured cracking the code to living life in the sighted world lay in observing these miraculous people in covert ways. The things I learned from their way of life made me question my way of seeing the world in which we coexist. Disability and adversity can allow an individual to develop abilities that can take them to a whole new realm of existence. My new realm was that of pure beauty. So I began to focus on how I experienced the world in comparison to others.

Apparently, people can see ants walking on the concrete, birds flying in the sky and even individual blades of grass. I can only translate this as grey underneath their feet and floaters in their eyes, a blue haze above their head when they look up and a blanket of green that never ends. They talk about how cars look different, houses have character and ducks swim on water. I think they mean blurry noisy covered engines zooming past on a dull surface, shadowy stationary colours that feel odd or inviting, and that running water must be hitting something to make those quacking noises.

The world is a mysterious place. At what point is it acceptable to stop sighted people in their tracks and ask, 'Are you hallucinating?'

These are the same people who can find a glass on a table with eyes, not hands. These are probably the same people who recognize a person by sight and not sound. There are others who read subtitles on a film at a cinema and not need auditory description. Some can even look at food and know what it is without having to smell it. Seeing double (which has now turned to triple) blurry, vaguely coloured, rough-shaped objects is not the norm. I've been living as an imposter in the sighted world for the last four decades. Do you think it's too late to tell people what I really see?

Here's an example: at what point do you admit to someone you've known most of your life that you've never really seen their face? (Other than zoomed to 600 per cent on a computer screen – and then I can only really see outlines). Is there ever a right moment to tell an old school friend that you only recognize them by the vague colour of their coat, their voice and unique footsteps? That you used to hate the beginning of a new school term because you'd have to match masses of new coats to the names of the blurs wearing them? And yet, living in this constant problem-solving world has allowed me to look beyond the mass of atoms that appear to be there. I'm not sure that I could see past these atoms if my eyes worked as effectively as my intuition.

The beauty that exists in my blind world is so hard to put into the hazy words appearing on my screen right now. So, when someone asks me what it's like to be blind and what I can see, it's so hard to explain. Giving the usual answer of triple visions, vaguely coloured blurs and blobs does not mean much to the sighted person. Telling someone that green shadowy haze I can see is really grass (as that's what my brain's telling me) doesn't really help them, either. When they talk of blades of grass, I search my memory bank to remember what it felt like to pick fresh-smelling blades of lightweight grass to know what they mean. I am often told by sighted people that they can't imagine what it's like to be blind. The problem I think lays in that exact statement. Imagination can sometimes be hampered by sight.

Growing up in a world from which I felt detached gave me the gift of living with my imagination: thoughts became my knowledge and my intuition became my truth. Always alert to everything around me, I was rarely bored. Change in the world is inevitable, so an open mind was my only ally. I know that hostility is futile, as it only leaves me feeling bitter while the world carries on, carefree with life. Most of all, I know that I'm connected to something much bigger than anything that I can physically see; I belong to the universal energy that connects all living beings, and this is the most beautiful place to be.

While people whizz around panicking and creating drama, I feel safe in my feeling of stillness, in accepting life as it is. Walking past the most beautiful blur in the world has the same effect on me as walking past what a sighted person may call a hideous-looking blur. A blur is a blur. It's my intuition and a mix of our energies as we pass that tells me if this person is beautiful or not. Judging by appearance is a totally alien concept. Everyone always looks perfect to me, just as they are. How can imperfections exist in visual form? Surely it's only imperfect thinking that causes this negative judgement. Hearing people judging others on appearance alone always leaves me with a sinking feeling in my gut. The heart is a better judge than the eyes can ever be.

Every 'now' is a new creation; our power always lies in the present moment. Things happen, people change and situations disappear. Without sight, you learn to listen, to forgive and to love unconditionally. Nobody is here by chance; you're reading these words at exactly the time you need to see them. It's no accident that you're experiencing things in life as you are while the person next to you is spared. The argument that you had with a friend last week may have needed to happen. Whether you're in or out of work, you're positioned so the doors of opportunity can open to you with divine right timing. We never do things by accident; we just accidentally think that we're doing things wrong. I've learned to love living in this space, surrendering to something that's bigger than the human brain can ever comprehend.

Would my life be the same if I had sight? I am not sure that it would. For those short yet lengthy months that I had a little more vision, I became focused on things that really didn't matter. I began to look at the vague outline of people's faces as if it defined who they were. I'd watch a hazy TV show without hearing the true meaning behind it. I began looking at clothes and matching them in my head to a tribe of humans who'd wear them. I began to forget that everyone I met was a beautiful soul and started wondering if they were looking at me in an odd way because of something I'd done. I realized that I'd stopped being me.

It can be so easy to slip into the 'poor me' mindset when life changes happen, and I get that. However, I wasn't going to slide into the sticky pit of negative feelings when what I really wanted to do was fill in the pit – and stop others falling into it. As a school counsellor and play therapist, I understand how this can happen. I know that feelings are reactions to rehearsed scripts and scenarios in the mind. My scripts have always been positive, because I choose positivity. If we have no control over a situation, we do have a choice about how we feel about it. We're the sum of our experiences, and I knew at this time that, although my experience of Marfan syndrome had been mixed, here I was, still alive. And that's magic.

It's very rare to go through life without facing any health challenges. Illnesses can go as quickly as they come. Our physical health may fluctuate dramatically over a short period of time, and our mental health, too – like riding a rollercoaster. Our overall wellbeing is rarely static throughout our life's journey. Yet what are we meant to do when life changes for the worst, long term?

Some conditions have been healed via a non-medical route, with natural remedies, powerful positive thinking and prayer. Then there are those who have healed through medical intervention alone: either way, healing is such an amazing gift. But what about those who can't physically heal? The ones who are born with congenital abnormalities, birth defects and disabilities? Those with limbs missing, disorders of whole body systems, or severe immune disorders? While the gift of physical healing may not be possible in these cases, there can certainly be spiritual and mental healing – when you know how. Living with a disability, illness or health condition can be a more positive experience than you might think.

Research has found that many individuals who are born with adverse health conditions tend to have a higher level of resilience, a more positive outlook on life and higher levels of motivation overall than those born in perfect health. It's harder to be born in perfect health and suffer ill-health later in life. A loss of identity, adapting to a new way of life and societal reactions to you can all impact greatly upon your resilience, outlook on life and motivation to heal. If, however, you're born with adverse health conditions, you know no difference. You can't lose what you've never had. This is not to say that many do not struggle with living with health issues and many do, especially during certain stages in life. Seeing peers achieve things while you deal with certain restrictions due to physical or mental challenges is not easy. Where there's a will, though, there will always be a way. The beauty in your life should not depend upon your physical limitations.

If you've ever read about Stephen Hawking's outlook on life, you will get what that 'way' is. From a perfectly healthy person's perspective, Stephen Hawking may appear to have had a life-limiting disability, but he did not see it like that. This is what he had to say about disability:

If you're disabled, it's probably not your fault, but it's no good blaming the world or expecting it to take pity on you. One must have a positive attitude and must make the best of the situation that one finds oneself in; if one is physically disabled, one can't afford to be psychologically disabled... I find that people in general are very ready to help, but you should encourage them to feel that their efforts to aid you are worthwhile by doing as well as you possibly can.[1]

Such a profound mind can't be wrong. Living with a disability does not have to be as debilitating as you might think. As Hawking says, if you live with a physical disability you can't afford to develop a psychological one. The two can coexist in many disabilities but where possible, a positive mental attitude can prevent psychological disorders developing. We all choose how we wish to perceive

---

[1]   Hawking, S. 'Handicapped People and Science', *Science Digest* 92, No. 9 (September 1984).

the world, regardless of what is going on in our physical bodies. Not only is it important to look at the glass half-full instead of half-empty, but it's also humbling to remember to be thankful that you have a glass to begin with. Stephen Hawking does not have to be the exception to the norm.

Even when you're living with a disability or a health condition, there's always something positive that can be taken from it. I can always see beauty in situations in which many may struggle to see it. So, what can you can take from your own experience of health adversity? If you're one of the rare few who have never experienced any physical or mental health issues, then that's amazing. Fingers crossed it will remain like that. It's likely, however, that you've experienced something in relation to your health that has been less than ideal. Even if it was a bad case of the flu when you were a young child, there will have been a lesson in there somewhere for you. You just may not know it yet. This is the message of this book: regardless of your health story, you can always change the script to a positive one. Becoming one with a negative script only gives you a negative sequel. Is this what you really want to be remembered for?

Telling our story is important, but is only as important as the next person's. We're bombarded daily by social and mainstream media with stories of suffering. Rarely a day goes by without stories of an increase in depression rates or fatal risks to health due to the consumption of certain products. Fear-based health news will always attract attention from individuals who can easily get sucked into this fear lair – and it can be hard to escape it. What many of us don't realize, however, is that we have a choice to stay away from this fear-lair. So much of our health can be controlled by looking after ourselves and keeping healthy if we wish to do so. Looking after our mental health is just as important as looking after our physical health (although the media will have us believe that the world has become a mental-health mess). As Hawking stated, we need to maintain our psychological health when faced with physical health challenges. For me, the way to do this is through positive thinking.

Optimists always have more fun as they choose to see the good in life and all that it provides. Optimists don't have the perfect life; they just choose to see perfection in life. If we see fear, we create more of the same. We always have a choice about what to give our power to, so we're never truly powerless. If you live with adverse health, that's not enough to stop you from seeing the beauty in life. It may be hard living in a body with physical limitations, but it does not have to limit your life. Learning to love ourselves regardless of our imperfections is the best present that we can ever give ourselves. How boring would the world be if we were flawless clones, just the same as the next person? (In Chapter 9, I offer exercises to challenge the perceptions of beauty; *see pages 179–193.*)

Choosing not to see problems and to start seeing opportunities is so freeing on every level imaginable. The thing with problems and problematic thinking as opposed to positive thinking is that there's always a pay-off when problems are involved – which is why some people do not see the world in a positive light. The ego loves a bit of drama, and the best way to get into drama is to slip into the 'poor me' mindset. I think it's fair to say that almost everyone has been dragged into or willingly leaped into some form of drama in life at one time or another. That's human nature. When we're in this drama triangle of Victim, Perpetrator and Rescuer, there's always a pay-off to the ego along the way. This is not to say that we do drama intentionally, but it does happen and it makes the ego happy. Even by doing simple things such as replacing the words 'I suffer from...' with 'I am successfully living with...' can halt the ego and ignite your true self and a love of life. (For more on this, see the six-step AFLOAT exercise in Chapter 10, which invites you to change suffering into successful living.)

Learning to love your imperfections can arise in many ways. Have you ever thought that sharing your life history and your health issue(s) can help people feel connected – people who may have been feeling isolated before you spoke with them? Becoming a mentor to a young person, for example, with the same condition as you could help them see that life may not be as limited as they thought. Starting a support group in your local area to help fundraise and raise awareness of your medical condition can take minimal effort, yet make a huge impact on a local and global scale. Starting to write a blog, creating vlogs or writing a book spreads your positive message of hope to people across the world. We never really get to know how our everyday actions can be recorded as historical events until after those events. Change starts with an idea; it gains support, influences people and leads to changes in legislation. Everyone has a message to spread, and positive change has one thing in common: it begins with someone like you. (To dive deeper into your own story and explore how you might write it, see Chapter 11.)

When you get into that positive, blissful place of beauty, be prepared. Of course, you can't prepare for surprises, but I want you to know that amazing, unexpected opportunities can arise. Here's just one example.

After so long living in my own little blind bubble, there came a time when I had to admit to both myself and the outside world that I needed a little assistance. To continue living independently, I'd have to use a white cane. When this was not enough to stop my falls, bumps and bruises, I took a bitter pill for my pride and realized that I needed a guide dog. The universe certainly gave me an amazing surprise when I was gifted my extraordinary guide dog, Munch (who I introduce in Chapter 4). I realized that surrendering to what I needed at that moment was a positive; it bought me a special gift from the universe. Regardless of all the negatives of ill-health and disability, there can be a positive.

The universe holds the bigger picture of our lives, while we may just know the smaller, day-to-day picture. When you feel connected to the beauty of the universe, you get to see like the universe. You begin to trust and accept yourself. If something doesn't feel right at this precise moment it does not mean that it will never feel right; it's okay not to have perfection, not to be perfect. The message is to really listen to that intuitive voice within. That's how I knew when the time was right to apply for my guide dog; it was the perfect time for Munch to come into my life. Of course, planning ahead and thinking how you want your life to change for the better is a positive step, as you're planting the seeds for future growth.

Yet we need to listen to our own internal voice to know when we need to act and when not to act. This knowing can help transform a life of limitations into a life of opportunity.

Use the power of positive thought and you will see the beauty in your own difference in a way that you may never have noticed before. When you see this beauty, you empower yourself, rather than disempower yourself in a victim role. Empowerment is such a freeing feeling. I often think how Paralympians are not born with special powers; it's their sheer motivation, hard work and optimism that empowers them to become exceptional athletes regardless of adversity. They embrace their uniqueness. The world will be a far better place when we all learn to embrace and love the beauty in our differences.

So here's the story, from childhood to 'Guide Dog Gift Day' and beyond (I've included exercises and visualizations to try, too, in Chapters 8–11). I forgot to mention that sight loss is only a minor part of the medical condition I have, but I keep forgetting that, too. Learning to love who you are and uncovering your own strengths in your health adversity is such an empowering place to be.

I hope that this book helps you find and appreciate your own blissful bubble of uniqueness.

———

CHAPTER 2

From Small Blur to Big Blur

Moving hands? Moving hands?

How can this man sit here and tell me that I can only see moving hands? Okay, well, it's my mind not my eyes telling me that this blur in front of me is a man, and he must be sitting on a chair, otherwise he's hovering in mid-air. Which would be impressive, but a bit freaky at the same time.

Back to this moving hand thing.

'Well, I can see things, I just can't read far,' I blustered, trying to convince the ophthalmologist. Even that was a bit of an exaggeration as my usual rule of 'If I sniff it I can see it' (meaning it looked like I was trying to inhale a form of Braille to decipher the print on the page) had gone out of the window for the last year or so. But I just kept forgetting to go and get it checked out.

My double vision had increased to triple vision over time, which to be honest was more amusing than scary. The only way I can explain triple vision is to liken it to a scene from the 1980s TV show, *Sesame Street*. I recall a popular scene – children moving around on the screen with special-effect auras streaming after them. Now that may have looked scary to anyone with perfect vision, but as I was born with partial sight, things like this were normal to me. And how could I fear what was normal?

On the plus side, moving hands meant at least I was seeing something. Unless, of course, you mistake it for another object. My firework mind flips back to my loving grandmother who had a huge influence on me as I was growing up. She was a true Earth angel whom I admired greatly. I remember her telling me one day that she'd stood by her kitchen window, as she did most mornings, and saw three boys across the road waiting by the bus stop. Well, at least she thought they were boys standing there. Every morning she waved at them until the bus came. It was only by chance that one morning she happened to glance again at the bus stop after she heard the bus drive off. She became a little confused when she realized that the boys were still there waving at her, as they should have been on the bus. After looking a little closer, she only then realized that 'the boys' were in fact trees and the 'waving hands' were the branches. We laughed for ages afterwards when she explained that she thought these boys were ever so polite for waving at her non-stop. See, moving hands (or branches in this case) can be a very welcoming thing.

Back to my hovering blur or, as the fully sighted would say, the ophthalmologist on the chair. There I sat in this man's office listening to his voice change to a sympathetic tone, which I presumed was meant for me. The words that floated out of his mouth drifted towards my ever-vigilant ears and began sending alien messages to my brain. These sympathetic messages were those I'd heard many times before from the sighted world but never really paid attention to. They were not welcome and did not belong to my psyche. Messages of sympathetic loss, which I really didn't get; messages of pitiful vulnerability and the challenging adaptations that would be required; and that I needed to be fixed by possible future operations if I were to have a chance to live in a 'normal manner'. I heard all these words but did not accept them. I could understand why this lovely, kind man was telling me all this, but the truth within me didn't need to hear recycled platitudes. I was fine as I was.

Being partially sighted from birth really does give you an advantage in the resilience and problem-solving field. When you constantly use your other senses to support your lack of vision, there's never a time that fear of the unknown can ever enter your mind. You live the unknown day in, day out, so when I was told that the little sight I had was rapidly decreasing, there was no need for fear. The ophthalmologist's well-intended words did not scare me, because I had then, and have now, enough tools in my toolbox of life to know that everything will be okay just as it is. We're never given anything in this life that we can't cope with, and we're always where we're meant to be at exactly the right time. I truly believe that.

The blessing of being blind or having partial sight means I always feel connected to the unseen world. Growing up feeling isolated from the 'seeing' world has given me many bonuses. Not being able to see what others were laughing at gave me imagination; I had to be able to imagine what was so funny. Not seeing facial expressions gave me the opportunity to sense the energy of a person and develop my intuition on a greater scale than if I'd had to rely on my vision alone. An inability to see faces has given me an open heart and the ability not to judge anybody on appearance – in my eyes, everyone is perfect just as they are. Not being able to see what was written on the blackboard at school allowed my ears to be extra vigilant to what the teacher was saying and I developed great acting skills, too, pretending to write down what was apparently on the board until I could borrow a friend's book to copy up later.

Sight is a phenomenological thing; we can only know what sight means from our own viewpoint. We can never really get behind the eyes of another person to compare what we can see differently or alike. That's why it's hard to describe what I can and can't see. When I say 'see', it's about how my eyes and brain interpret the environment. Walking on a grey surface with blankets of green all around me with blurry, tall objects providing shelter from the sun means I am walking on a path with grass on either side and trees rooted firmly in the ground, providing shade. Now saying to people that I can see the grass is not really lying: what I mean is that I can see a bit of shadowy green. My brain interprets that as grass and tells my eyes, *I am looking at grass*. For the last four decades this is how I've operated, and it's all I know.

When individuals talk about being blind, or partially or fully sighted, there's far more complexity to this than first appears. When you've had sight loss since birth you have what I like to call 'Life Gain' to compensate. You see, life isn't all about what you can physically see around you – it runs much deeper, on a level that you can't imagine unless you've experienced it. There's an element of beauty in being disconnected from a mainstream life that seems to imprison so many of us these days. When you use only your eyes to get information to flood your brain, you can lose out on life's invisible secrets. When I hear the words 'You must be blind...' thrown around on TV shows, in songs or wherever by thoughtless people, I just smile sweetly, thankful for my blind bliss. I will take you to that place later, but for now, please trust me; it's not as weird as it might sound.

So, when the ophthalmologist told me that I'd lost more sight, I wasn't fearful of what even more reduced vision would mean. No, not really. I had so many coping mechanisms in place, it didn't occur to me to be frightened. The only bitter pill was that people would now realize how bad my vision really was, and my secret would be blown. Great.

When I started primary school, I recall sitting at a smooth-feeling desk on a chipped wooden chair attempting to look at all the new children around me. Having only had my two older brothers with me growing up and some friends who lived on the same street for reference, it was difficult to distinguish between my regular blurs and those new ones. I could easily recognize the voices of my brothers and the friends I already had, but this was a totally new experience that I knew was going to take a lot of getting used to. At four, I had to try to devise a system of relating these new-name children to their similar-looking blurred bodies in matching clothes. Not the easiest task for such a young child, especially in a new environment that kept tripping me up.

One of my earliest memories of primary school was being shouted at for colouring in a squirrel purple. (This was back in the early 1980s, when a stricter form of teaching was widespread in classrooms and compliance was a must. Not quite as harsh as the preceding decades, but still harsher than today's more compassionate way of teaching and encouraging the young.) I'd sat and looked at a faded photocopy of a squirrel, which I was told had to be coloured in the correct colour. I grabbed what I thought was a dark red wax crayon and began my artistic assault on this queer-looking image. I was well underway when I remember one of the children shouting at me to stop as I was doing it wrong. In true small-child fashion, he went to tell a teacher who came over and gave me the biggest row that I ever remember having. I was asked why it was the wrong colour and why it was so messy and outside the lines. The stinging tears that trickled down my cheeks were not just tears of embarrassment, but worst of all, tears of utter isolation. And so began my alien invasion of the sighted world.

The rest of the first year of my school life is a blur of uncomfortable memories of not fitting in and being overloaded with new sensory information that I had to piece together to be 'one of them'. I was a four-year-old dumped in the middle of a foreign community with people rushing past all sharing a love of life, yet here I sat in my own blurred bubble, separated from the rest of the world, unable to connect. I did not realize that I was even in this bubble; I just thought this was normal.

That first year in school, I was told I had a problem with my vision. This was during a routine eye examination, part of a compulsory check-up with the nurse. Until then, not even my parents knew that I had difficulty seeing even the most obvious things. It did, however, make sense to my grandmother, as she'd noticed that I could not see her when she picked me up from school. I still remember to this day standing by the huge blue school doors, feeling the chips in the wood and thinking how magical it was that all the children knew exactly the right time to head towards the school gates to meet their parents to go home. And how stupid I felt that I did not have that magical power. Ever the analytical thinker, I tried to work out if there was a pattern to it. I remember trying to work out who left after whom and tried to recall my place in process. It was after being called back for the umpteenth time after blissfully heading towards the school gate that I realized it didn't quite work like that. It was back to the drawing board as to how I was meant to know when to leave.

During this routine eye examination at school, my mother was told that my vision test result was much lower than it should have been and that I needed glasses. My mother was also told that there was something more serious going on with my health than extreme short-sightedness. After a careful eye examination, they found that the lenses of my eyes were subluxated (dislocated), which would have occurred at birth. Subluxation of the lenses is rare, and it's the result of either trauma to the eyes or inherited genetic conditions. After further medical examinations I was given the diagnosis of Marfan syndrome, a connective tissue disorder that can affect the eyes, heart, lungs, bones, joints, ligaments, skin and most of the body in differing ways. This was a shock to the family, especially as one of my brothers was also diagnosed at the same time as me.

After our diagnoses, it was later discovered that my father had Marfan syndrome, too. He'd always struggled with his eyesight, but because his work was mostly manual, he hadn't needed to read much. He'd gone through nearly three decades of life without anyone picking up that he had Marfan's, and would have continued that way had it not been for the thorough examination that I received and the diagnoses for the rest of the family. For this I am eternally grateful, as many individuals with Marfan syndrome die prematurely without medical intervention if complications arise. At a time of no internet, research into this strange condition was not readily available and so the numerous questions that must have been swimming around my parents' heads could only be answered by the conveyor belt of specialists who began passing through.

Fast-forward a few years and I'm standing in the queue waiting for the school dentist. I'm holding a pink piece of paper with my details on. The squiggles that I focus in on are obviously some sort of rushed writing. Focusing was struggle enough, but trying to read it? Impossible! My friend standing behind me asks to have a look at my pink paper as she sees that I can't make out what is written on it. Then she picks up on the 'medical conditions' section of the form. My friend manages to decipher the rushed written words 'Marfan syndrome'. I am standing in the school corridor waiting to be seen by a dentist, who I don't know or recognize by her clothes, and my friend utters the words, 'Urrgh! What is *that*?', pointing at the words 'Marfan syndrome'. At that point, I feel the loneliest I've ever felt.

Looking back, I know that she didn't mean to say it in a harsh way. She was my friend, after all, and to an eight-year-old child it must have been quite scary to think that someone has something that's a little 'odd'. But her questioning continued not just on that day but also for some time afterwards, which felt like an eternal inquisition. One of the most torturous questions she asked was, 'Are you still one of us?'

My alien invasion of the 'normal' world began to feel more intense. Yet deep down, although I was feeling like an outsider in a close-knit world, I did have a powerful sense that everything was going to be okay. Something inside me knew that if I relied on myself I could get through anything in life.

The rest of primary school went by in a muddled mess. Two further incidents made me feel that my alien invasion may have been exposed. The first was overhearing two teachers talk about me right in front of me (professionalism at its worst).

Just after my diagnosis of Marfan syndrome, I remember playing on the floor with the other children at school. I was much taller than all the others in my class, which can make a child feel like the odd one out. As I ran around after the children I heard one of the teachers say in a pitying tone, 'She does look different to the others; she is all legs and arms.' I remember thinking what a weird thing to say about me. I now realize that they must have been told about the muscular-skeletal characteristics of Marfan syndrome and were commenting on how tall and thin I was. Those words, which I knew were not meant in a nasty way, made me feel even more isolated in an already very lonely world.

The other time that the unprofessional, absent-minded adult world spoke about me like I wasn't there was when a social worker came to my house not long after the diagnosis to talk about my educational needs. I remember sitting on the floor with my brother playing with toys when a rather heated discussion erupted between the social worker and my mother about the possibility of me going to a 'specialist school'. The specialist school was some 20 miles away. There, I'd be assisted with my education by having one-to-one help.

Now, my mother is a very quiet woman who does not do confrontation at all, but where the family is concerned she becomes a whole different person, almost ninja-like. It's comical to watch: a 4ft 11in placid lady turning into a machine! As the social worker walked her black fitted suit towards the door, my mother trailed behind her telling her that I wouldn't be going to any other school and that I'd remain in my current school with my two brothers. As a result of this, she wouldn't need to see the woman again, so she wished her well. To this day I think that was the best decision ever made for me, as I know that if I'd gone to a school for the sight impaired I wouldn't be the strong, resilient, resourceful woman that I am today. For that, I thank my ninja-like mamma bear.

Just as I'd become used to the number of steps needed between my primary school classrooms and recognising the teachers by their footsteps, it was time to go to secondary school. I never really dreaded this, although I was anxious about how I was going to find everything and how was I going to read all the new information that I'd need. During primary school, my friends had whispered into my ear what I needed to copy down from the board or overhead projector, or I'd copy from their notes when the teacher wasn't looking. I did wonder if it would be possible for me do this at the new school.

On my first day in secondary school I remember crying when I lost my classmates and got totally lost in the school and didn't know where to go. Luckily, I saw one of my brothers (or rather he saw me), who directed me to where I needed to go. To me this was such a failure, as I'd methodically planned out in my head ways of coping with this change when I got to the school. I'd visited it once before and used memory to take in as much information as possible, such as where the steps were so as not to fall on them, and to learn the door numbers at the beginning of each corridor so that I'd be able to count along the doors to find the classroom I needed. During my last few months of primary school, I'd also casually asked people who went to the school about its layout.

Looking back, it was quite impressive for an 11-year-old to have this much forward planning. On that first day, however, I'd forgotten to remain in lighthouse-keeper mode and momentarily lost concentration, which led to me not knowing where the hell I was. From that day forward, I always kept alert to my surroundings and used even the most minute detail, such as the feeling of the surface of the ground under my feet, to help me track where I was so that my memory would have this imprint to help with future routes.

Apart from the usual name-calling, distraction techniques to get out of written work I couldn't see, a few falls and feeling more alien-like as the years went on, the rest of my school life flew by. It still shocks me to this day how I got to the age of 16 without anyone knowing how bad my vision really was. I've been asked many times why I did not tell the teachers that I could not see and get help, but in mainstream education sight loss was still hugely misunderstood in the 1980s through to the 90s.

And also, as I said previously, you can't see things that you don't know exist. If there's a poster on a wall but I can't see that there's a poster there, then how can I tell somebody that I can't see it? I take ownership of the fact, however, that when you get so far into your own secret, there comes a point at which it's almost impossible to tell your secret. I was aware at a very young age that when I told someone that I couldn't see, they never quite understood how severe this was, as to others I seemed to function perfectly well on my own. What they didn't realize was that I'd devised my own coping strategies since a young child, covering up the fact that I couldn't see just to fit in.

When I was 11, my mother wrote a note to my maths teacher saying that I could not see the blackboard. The problem appeared to be resolved in the teacher's mind by moving me to the front of the class. I still couldn't see. There was a shine on the blackboard from the windows; the white chalk wasn't bold enough, and the blackboard was grey, not black (when I read, I need a black background with white type). For an 11-year-old to then tell the teacher that she still could not see, even from the front desk, which was probably only three or four feet away, would have not gone down well. So there I sat, looking up and pretending to copy things down while inside my self-confidence shrivelled like grapes to raisins.

A blessing came in the sixth form when I chose to do GNVQs (vocational qualifications), which meant mostly self-supported study. I was so happy to be able to work from workbooks because I could use my 'sniff to see' rule – putting my face really close to the page – and I ended up with distinctions at levels 2 and 3. My passion for learning grew, as I knew I had the ability to achieve great things if I relied on my own methods of learning rather than the old-fashioned copying down of information from boards and projectors.

Probably one of the scariest times in my life was when I could see slightly better than I'd ever been able – bizarre but true. After another failed eye operation, it was suggested that I try wearing contact lenses as surgeons had removed the lens from one of my eyes. In theory, a contact lens might give me vision that I'd never had. From birth my lenses were subluxated, so I'd never been able to see in focus. Therefore, when I had surgery to remove it, it was suggested that maybe a contact lens would work instead. I complied with the doctors and went ahead with the operation. At that time I'd been taken on as a student nurse in psychiatric nursing, and they were aware that the planned operation could give me the sight I needed to start my career.

As I awoke from the operation, I was assured that it had been a success. I took my bandaged eye home with the rest of my body and sat and waited for the miracle of sight. When I realized my sight was worse than before the operation, I questioned the surgeon, only to be told it was all perfectly normal – they were just waiting for the eye to settle down and it would be fine. Yet the moment I'd awoken from the anaesthetic, I had a feeling deep within me that was still there in the pit of my stomach. This feeling warned me against everything I was being told.

Ever the optimist, I persevered with the contact lens even though my eye really didn't like it. I had infections and irritations for four months until enough was enough and I stopped wearing it. I have to say I was relieved, as it was the weirdest time of my life. It was like living in a fantasy world where everything was so vivid and out of proportion that I felt I was in a constant dream state. I could see outlines of birds on the ground, which I'd never been able to see before, and the texture of grass, not just a blanket of green on the floor. Yet the structure of my eye, married to a painful, intrusive lens, was to lead to a serious separation. They would never again reunite.

After persistently questioning the medical team who worked with my ophthalmic surgeon, I was finally told of the complications that were stopping me from being able to see. I had post-operative inflammation and oedema on the retina, so it was decided that the lens would be taken out. I was to be left with no lens or contact lens, so my vision would be worse than before. Luckily, they had operated on my worst eye, so at least my 'good' eye would be able to give me some colour and light perception.

This level of vision, however, wouldn't be good enough to allow me to continue with my nursing studies. My nursing career had been chucked away just as my faulty lens had. It was okay, though; I felt no sadness, just a sense of relief, as the last thing I'd ever want to do is cause harm to another human being due to a mistake I might have made because of my poor vision.

The only sadness I did feel was around the lack of an explanation – I was never given the reason why the operation didn't work and why I had the complications afterwards. I asked on numerous occasions to see the consultant who had operated on my eye, but was not allowed to see him even though he was there in the clinics I attended. I am a practical-minded woman who needs answers to questions, and to this day no ophthalmologist can say what went wrong and caused that irreversible damage.

So, there I was back to square one, worse off than I'd ever been. On the plus side, I'd never see those freakishly large birds that the sighted claim they see each day. I hear their sweet tweets and chirpy chirps in the sky, and imagine tiny multicoloured feathered friends flying around in a glittery twirl, pooping out rainbow-coloured rose petals. Come on, which world would you prefer to live in? I know which one I happily inhabit.

It was only during my counselling training in 2003 that I received adequate help with written work. Everything was enlarged, and I always received a printed and digital copy of the work from the whiteboard before each lecture. The relief that this brought me was immense. At the age of 26, I finally felt like I belonged in a classroom environment.

Yet there's a time in every secret club when something slips out and alerts others that you're not really who you seem to be. That day came in my thirty-eighth year of life.

CHAPTER 3

The Day It All Changed

I woke up to the sound of the alarm on my phone and followed its melodic tune to try to locate where I'd dropped it the night before. After finding its vibrating shell, it was time to hit the snooze button just a couple more times. I turned onto my side and looked forward into the mirrored wardrobe to see a vague outline of an oddly shaped blob in the bed, which I guessed was me. After opening the window to hear if it was raining, I felt for the wardrobe to pick out what clothes I should wear. Being guided by my sensitive fingertips and by the colours of the clothes, I recalled what I'd bought over the last few years. I blindly picked out weather-appropriate clothing after searching my memory bank for what I owned. After feeling for labels, seams and buttons to work out if they were the right way around, I dressed and hoped for the best.

I started my way across the landing and picked up a stray pair of trousers that had become looped around my foot. I mean, what better place for one of the kids to leave dirty clothes than outside their blind mother's room? As I felt around to reach my sons' bedroom door to call the little monsters, I heard my younger son's walrus-like snore and my elder son's fart. From these auditory clues, I knew that they'd not been abducted by aliens overnight and were safe and sound. Waking them up for the thirty-ninth time in 10 minutes, they finally sat up, looking like the nicest blurry outlines any parent could lay eyes on. Having finally received a verbal response from the half-awake, half-comatose boys, it was time to leave their boy-smelling room and carefully side-step the other obstacles they'd left on the landing. After knocking on my daughter's bedroom door, I entered the room to an explosion of clothes, make-up and paraphernalia strewn across the floor.

After going downstairs and picking up the food I'd prepared the night before, I chucked it all into my bag ready for work, then asked my eldest daughter, Rasheena, to make sure the boys got ready for school. As I gathered up my work stuff as gracefully as an old oaf, I thought today was going to be like any other day.

Reaching down to feel what shoes I had on (thank God for different textures), I checked I was semi-presentable to the world and headed out the door. Through the darkness of the early morning, I traced my well-rehearsed steps for half a mile to the train station, never losing concentration as I danced the curves of the pavements and paused for my heel to tap the back of the kerb to know it was safe to step into the road.

I'd learned the hard way that losing concentration when walking along in the dark could have painful consequences. Early one Christmas Eve, when I was rushing to catch a bus to the nearest city to buy last-minute gifts, I stupidly zoned out from what I was doing and forgot to count my steps. With hands in pockets and walking at a speed that I'm sure sent smoke from my heels, I forgot all about the pavement and did what can only be described as a hop, skip and a jump into the road. After landing painfully yet hilariously on my side as if I were lounging across a car bonnet for a photo shoot, I lay in the road unable to move – with one leg beneath me and my hands stuck firmly in my pockets. With cut-up knees and a hole in my trousers, I swiftly got up and hobbled along to the bus stop pretending nothing had happened. The moral of this story is never to walk with my hands in my pockets (just as my grandmother used to tell me), but also more importantly, never, *ever* to zone out of my well-rehearsed, almost robotic way of getting around.

Back to the journey in hand, and I arrived at the train station without scabby knees (always a bonus). Luckily, I live in a town where only five trains run daily and there's just one platform, so the fear of getting on the wrong train didn't enter my mind. I'd been doing this journey for the last four years, so I knew everything there was to know about timing the lead-up to the train's arrival. Ten minutes beforehand, a rumbling, large-sounding van bumped along the main road, regular as clockwork. A mother in a house behind the train station would lose her cool trying to get her kids ready for school. A heavy foot-stepping blob always walked past the station with keys jingling in his pocket. These were all refreshing auditory signs that the train was imminent. Next, I'd exchange morning greetings with the man who put the barriers down (it's a manned station and yes, they still exist). After he'd phoned through and I'd heard the click of the receiver on the wall-mounted phone, he would come to stand next to me. We'd talk about anything and everything. I loved these rail workers as they wore brightly coloured orange coats so I couldn't mistake them for lamp posts, rubbish bins or other random things dotted around the place. I'd started my day this way many times. I had no idea that this day would start or end any differently.

When I heard the train arrive and come to a halt, I put out my arm at exactly the right angle to locate the raised door button. I waited for the sound of the doors sliding open. My leg knew just how far to rise to find the first step up onto the train. I eagerly stepped aboard and discretely felt for a seat with my hands and feet, sitting as near to the exit as possible. I robotically arranged my bags where I could easily feel them and took out my purse, phone and headphones. After buying my ticket from the friendly conductor, I settled in for the 21-minute journey I knew off by heart. While listening to music, I stayed alert for the three stops that passed by and got ready to leave the comfort of the seat to stand up just as the train slowed down. As the train pulled into the station, I pretended to look casually around the carriage and wait for my fingers to gradually find the button to open the door, which was located at chest height. My fingers then rejected the closing arrows buttons and opted for the opening ones. Thank God buttons and such things are now raised, making it easier for people with sight problems to decipher differences.

I stepped off the train and walked the 27 steps to the exit I needed for my taxi. While I waited, I pretended to look at my phone, which I couldn't see. I heard the quiet purr of the engine and slow crunching of gravel as the taxi pulled up, so it was time to step into my white metal blob. I used a regular firm and I knew their habits as well as they knew mine; I got picked up where no other taxis tended to wait. That way, I'd have the right taxi and not scare some poor random driver with my morning ramblings.

Arriving at work, I entered a practically deserted school and felt the reception desk for the signing-in book. Rotating the book around so that the metal strip with dots on was on the right, I knew the book was facing the right way. I then felt for the rip-out slips and used the width of my fingers to gauge where I was meant to write my details. This, however, was not always a good enough cover; one time during a fire-alarm drill, the fire safety officer had looked at the book and realized that some random stranger had squiggled something in. Only through the process of elimination did they find out that it was me. After my mumblings of how sorry I was, and that I'd write better next time, I vowed to find a way to make my signature look more professional. That vow never had a chance to come to fruition.

I discreetly used the walls to guide me to find my way through the maze of the school and go up two flights of well-trodden stairs to get to my room. I pulled out my key and felt for the lock with my finger. With my other hand I turned the key the right way so that I could align the two to open the door. After dropping the key, I used my foot to feel for the sound of the key scraping on the polished floor. I retrieved it, and finally got in.

I set up my laptop with my electronic narrator and magnified inverted-colour screen then laid out all the things I'd need that day. I checked that the floor and surfaces areas were clutter-free, running my feet along the floor and my fingers across the worktops to memorize where everything was. Next, I left the room and became reacquainted with the smooth, newly painted walls, tickling them lightly as I found my way to the link person's office to pick up my diary for the day (the 'link person' liaises between the school and the counselling service). Usually, he left it in the same place, but that day it was not there. So, I left without it and headed back to my room.

My day got off to a great start, with all my morning clients turning up. I loved being a counsellor as it was such a privilege to share in the stories that each client brought. Being of service to people and witnessing change in an individual was so humbling and rewarding. As the day went on, in between clients I attempted to write up notes on my chatty laptop, which insisted I was writing mumbo jumbo. I had triple vision and a lovely aura around my white writing on the black background, yet I was still convinced that I was right and the laptop was exaggerating the corrections I needed to make. After all, I couldn't let my guard slip now and show anyone, even my laptop, that I couldn't see what the hell was going on. What was I? Human? So I continued through the day – until one incident made me stop and think that maybe being a 'secret blind' may have to come to an end.

A client came to see me at lunchtime, which happened if an urgent appointment was needed. During my session with this client, there was a knock at the door. As I opened it and looked to my right, there stood the blurry outline of a child. As he started to speak, I began to panic – not because of what he was saying, but because I didn't recognize his voice. He asked if he could change his appointment to a later time that day, but I thought he was a client who had missed his appointment earlier on – and so I told him he would have to wait until the following day as I had no appointments left. He was such a quiet child and he sounded really confused. He went away and I felt terrible, but there was nothing else I could have done as I was fully booked all day. It was only when the link person dropped the diary off in my office later that lunchtime that I realized the mistake I'd made. I'd confused him with another boy of similar height and a practically identical voice.

The guilt that engulfed me afterwards was overpowering. This poor child did have an appointment after lunch and I could have changed him with someone else with hardly any hassle. As I can't see faces, I had to rely on voice recognition and match that with the name in the diary (which I used a magnifier to see). For the rest of the day I cursed myself for not being as alert as usual. I'd let my guard drop and rejected a child asking for help. I considered myself an emotionally intelligent person and I felt such guilt. It was only a small incident, and yet it was the final straw: I realized I was not able to carry on with my job.

I did manage to see the client at the end of the day for a shorter session and explained the confusion, but it still didn't feel enough. Mixing up people when you can't even see them may not seem like a big deal to anyone with sight, and most may think it's understandable. But for me, at that moment in time, it felt like the end of an era.

For the whole of my life I'd been able to cope with everything and had kept my terrible vision a secret. This had been a seemingly small incident, yet the enormity of it was devastating. I knew this was what I'd dreaded and had put off for so long. I now needed to be more honest with people about my vision. Even those closest to me didn't know how bad my sight was, as I'd always played it down and used coping strategies to get through it. I think what I dreaded more was that somehow, I'd now have to persuade people that my vision really *was* that bad. A fear of mine was that I wouldn't be believed. Even though I'd told a few people that my eyesight wasn't the best, if I hadn't fully admitted it to myself, then how would I admit it to others? This was going to hit my ego hard: I'd have to show my vulnerability.

This was the first time in my life I acknowledged that maybe I needed to seek help and learn not to be so fiercely independent. The hardest thing was that I felt that my independence was about to be stolen from me and there was nothing I could do to get it back. Everybody who knew me knew that I lived my life at a rapid pace and never limited myself. I lived life to the max and never stopped to think that I'd be the person to get in my own way, stopping me from succeeding.

That night, after doing the usual chores around the house and spending some time with the kids, I meditated on what to do. Meditation to me is the answer to everything in life and beyond. Having practised it for the last 14 years, it has become my inbuilt Google for all life's queries. That night's quest for clarity was probably one of the greater asks of my internal searching, yet it somehow felt the most freeing.

What came from that life-changing meditation was a total acceptance of a new way of living. The fear of losing my coping strategies was probably the greatest blow to my ego, which believed it could combat anything. I began to realize, however, that although I loved my life so much and always had, these coping strategies were hindering my life experiences. I'd always planned things methodically; I'd convinced myself I was spontaneous, yet really I wasn't. I may have been spontaneous in the fact that I loved a varied life, but each activity had an action plan prepared in advance so I could cover up any blunder I might make. My ego really took a bashing that night as I made some more uncomfortable discoveries about myself. I was not invincible. I was not being truly authentic and I'd become too dependent on my comfort zone. Things really needed to change.

That evening, I emailed my employer giving a month's notice – I knew I needed to finish work as it had all become too much for me. My eyesight was not the only issue, as Marfan syndrome had also given me many a health challenge that I'd just brushed off. In the last four years alone I'd been hospitalized with a bad case of pneumonia due to the weakness in my lungs and was back in work a week after being discharged, although I really shouldn't have been. I'd been admitted with a cardiac episode, yet kept it quiet from work. Multiple dislocations had seen me in full leg casts and braces of varying sizes, yet I still turned up to work, never wanting to be anything but strong. Due to scoliosis (curvature of the spine) I had many issues with protruding discs, yet still sat smiling at the client in front of me. I detested painkillers and would much rather use breathing techniques and visualizations to get through difficult times. Marfan syndrome is never kind to its host.

After the email was sent, I felt a sense of blissful release. This would be the first time in my adult life that I wouldn't work, volunteer or study, yet I knew I had no choice but to give up work for a while to be able to readjust to my rapidly failing eyesight. Yet that feeling of failure and all the doom and gloom it brought only actually lasted for a couple of hours, and it soon gave way to a feeling of relief and happiness. The happiness came from the fact that I could now stop pretending to the outside world and plan my next steps. I loved solving problems. My analytical brain could work through all the emotions, then spring into action. I've always been quite male-brained in the way I see the world: for every problem there's a solution, without fail.

Thirteen years previously I'd received some white-cane training – although I'd only attended one session as my embarrassment about being visually impaired was too much for my ego. I now needed to retrain to use the cane, but there were limits to using a cane alone. With a cane, the thing is that you can only be alert to what's directly ahead of you; there are no warnings of upcoming obstacles. For this reason, I felt that I needed to apply for a guide dog. This was an even bigger blow to the ego, but I knew I had to do it. I'd also have to become the dog lover that I'd never been. But I loved a challenge, and this would be one of the biggest yet.

I spent the rest of the month working on endings with my clients, whom I'd loved working with so much. Counselling children was such a rewarding job; children taught me so much about life and how they see the world. At times it was harrowing and other times, euphoric. Seeing a child grow and overcome seemingly impossible issues was such a fulfilling thing to witness. This was the only thing that was really keeping me from fully embracing my choice to leave work, but I knew that the counsellors taking over my case load would be amazing, giving the children the support they needed. The final month passed quickly and the ending felt natural as I finished the week before Christmas. I hoped the new year would bring fresh new opportunities.

Now that I'd finished work, I had mixed responses from an ever-judgemental society. I was left with a freeing yet restrictive case of leisure time. Having always been involved in studying, volunteering or working throughout my adult life, even when my children were small, this was the first time that I'd sat and wondered what my next step would be.

To reveal who I'd always been, deep down, but hidden in public was a confusing and challenging task. It's a bit like that moment when Superman's identity is revealed – instead of him peeping out now and again during his everyday life, he becomes known only as Superman from then on. The secret becomes your new known identity.

I had to think a lot about everything I'd taken for granted. I knew that I couldn't see what others could, but I still didn't feel sight impaired. I knew that I could never drive, but I got around as well as anyone else. I could not recognize people or their facial expressions, but I could hear the smiles that they gave out. I could not see the landmarks from the bus I was travelling on, but I could feel and then memorize the bends on the roads to alert me to my upcoming stop. With all this in mind, I always questioned if my sight loss could even be classed as a disability. My abilities far outweighed my lack of ability. Well, this is what my reasoning mind had been telling me for almost four decades, so to be told any differently was really knocking my ego into shape and giving it a bit of a tantrum.

I've never been ashamed of my sight impairment, but I'd never actually identified myself with it, either. I've always felt that we humans are far greater than the bodies we dwell in. This is by no means denying the impact that the body and ailments can have on an individual, but I'd always seen my sight loss as a tool for empowerment, as a way to reach a purposeful potential.

When I applied for my guide dog I was advised that the application process would be lengthy. The wait for such an amazing, well-trained dog was very long due to high demand and the high cost of training. Guide dogs come from a charity that helps the blind and partially sighted, and there are different stages to go through to assess whether a guide dog rather than cane training is the best option for the individual. One of the stumbling blocks I first encountered before turning my informal request into a formal application was to get over my assumption that I was 'not really a dog person'. Now don't get me wrong, I love animals. I am vegan and only buy products not tested on animals, but I can't say I am a natural animal person, and dogs have always frightened me to a certain degree. Growing up, I had a dog whom I loved, but I've always had my reservations about wholly trusting a dog. This was an obvious issue to deal with, but I realized quite quickly that a dog would be a much nicer option than taking a cane. I reasoned with myself that a guide dog would also be a little kinder on the eye. On the downside, a dog would be a little messier to clean up after.

From the limited number of people who knew I was waiting for a guide dog came a variety of reactions. The sympathetic ones tended to rush to help with anything from packing shopping to asking if I needed things reading out or explained to me. This was sweet if not somewhat scary, as my independence was being shaken a little. *Was this a sign of things to come?* I wondered. *How would life change now that I was 'officially' losing my sight?* The second group of people, the bewildered ones, tended to fall into two categories: the first were those who tried to catch me out. Oh yes, they did that, trust me. I had people purposely drop things in front of me then wait to see if I'd pick them up. I even had a much-loved friend tell me, 'It's stupid that you have to give up work. If David Blunkett (the former MP) can work, you should be able to.' Hmm, if a friend whom I loved dearly said that, then there wasn't much hope! Yet I really did understand where people were coming from, as they only looked at things in black and white. The second lot of bewildered individuals were outraged that there was not enough help around for me to be able to continue working.

What they didn't get was the time I needed to adjust to this way of living myself. I knew that everything would be okay, but for the time being I just needed a bit of breathing space to find my own solutions to the difficulties I was having in my everyday life.

So here I was, patiently waiting for my neon sign to show that I belonged to a group in society that nobody really understood. With a guide dog at my left side wherever I went, my Mrs Invisible mask would have to come off. No more sneaking around on the outskirts hoping not to be noticed. My sidekick and I would be out in public for all to see.

I patiently waited to re-emerge into the world as a duo and, I was soon to discover, this patience would certainly pay off.

CHAPTER 4

When Two Odd Socks Make a Matching Pair

With a hyped-up teenager and an equally hyped-up granddaughter squealing away in the background, I picked up the ringing house phone and was greeted by the voice of an angel. Her words set me off on one of the biggest highs ever.

Only that morning, I'd been wondering when the guide dog office would get in touch with me about my dog. Here was the answer, loud and clear down the phone. I don't mean to blow my own trumpet; I do manifest what I want in life – but even I was shocked at how quickly this had come about.

As the trainer talked into my excited ear, I realized that my prayers had not only been answered, but were also blessed to the max. As this life-changing conversation continued, I giggled inwardly as she described the dog she had in mind. By the sound of it, this was certainly the right dog for me.

Up until this point I'd thought that golden or black Labradors and German Shepherds were the stereotypical guide dogs. I knew different breeds were available, but I sensed that mine would be unique. About a month prior to this day I'd had a weird but enlightening dream: my dog was half-fish (Nemo from *Finding Nemo*) and half-dog (Doodles from *The Tweenies*). In this dream I kept saying to the guide-dog charity that although I was extremely grateful to have the dog, I was a bit puzzled as it didn't look like a typical guide dog. They kept reassuring me that it was a dog, and a very special dog at that. From this dream, I knew that my real-life dog wouldn't be typical, either.

As the trainer arranged to bring my new dog to meet me to see if we were a match, I was drinking in a cocktail of emotions. I knew that I now had two remaining days as a guide dog-free, fumbling grandmother who walks like a penguin, invisible to the world. There was an element of sadness, too, as it felt like my independence was being stripped away: I'd now have to depend upon my guide dog. It felt like my coping strategies were becoming redundant, as new blood was coming to show me how things should be done. My cocktail of emotions, however, contained a far greater shot of positivity. I knew how blessed I was to be given such an amazing opportunity to meet my new adventure partner. I'd be able to go out again to places I'd avoided, so excitement was a large factor. The most intoxicating part of this, though, was knowing that my guide dog was not going to be of a traditional breed. Breaking the stereotypical image of what blind was, I needed to have a matching odd sock to make us a pair.

After putting the phone down, the first thought that came to mind was what people would think. As if by magic, my guide dog would soon appear – would they think I was lying about being blind? Assume that I'd stolen him from a poor blind person in dark glasses standing on the street corner, wondering where their dog had gone? Or would they just assume I'd found a sly way to take my own dog into shops, dishonestly dressing him in a guide-dog harness rather than tie him up outside? All these thoughts raced through my head as I tried to control my mad mind-mumbling.

My family were so happy when I gave them the news. The only person yet to be convinced was me. My life as a guide dog-free blind person was coming to an end, and in a couple of days I'd have what felt like a permanently attached extra limb by my left side. The mixed emotions I felt were nothing like I'd ever experienced – like being at the top of a rollercoaster holding on for dear life. There was no way back, as that meant taking everyone back with me too – which wouldn't have been fair. Clenching your fists at that crucial point before the drop, before the rush of excitement fills your body, you pray to get it over with. Yet you want to remain perched there for eternity, staying safe. So, what else is there to do in that precise moment but stop? To ponder that from now on, things would be different. To capture those last few moments until life would change forever.

I decided to go for a walk to savour the last time I'd officially be alone. As my training started in two days' time, this would be the last time I'd go out without my new dog. So off I went on a dark winter's night to the local supermarket. Not a big thing for most, but it's a bit of a challenge when you can't see what you're doing. It was only when I began walking in the most mindful way that I realized I hadn't been out on my own in around six months when it was this dark. It all came flooding back to me, trying to get around to and from work not being able to see and not telling anyone that I could not see – which had made it feel like a secret mission that might go terribly wrong at any moment. A fall, walking into someone or something, a missed turn in the road or pavement could stop me in my lost tracks if my concentration lapsed. As I got to my destination, I realized that I'd apologized to five different people on the way after nearly bumping into them. Fair play, only one of them tutted.

At the checkout, queuing up to pay for my goods, I overheard that emotive topic of conversation that people throw around in society daily. A lady in front of me who sounded middle-aged was chatting with the cashier, saying she'd just finished work and was looking forward to getting home. She then went on to say, 'I don't know how people who don't work can sit around and do nothing all day and afford to pay all the bills. I certainly couldn't live like that.' As her multiple glass bottles clunked from the conveyor belt into her shopping bag, she continued to talk about such people being a drain on society. Her voice became louder and seemed to be directed towards me, so I assumed she was attempting to engage me in the discussion. From her tone of voice, it seemed like she believed I was 'one of her gang' as she carried on with her rant to the cashier. If only she knew that this drain on society would love to be back in work and paying taxes; after all, I'd invested thousands of pounds on my education to qualify me to do my work.

Standing there she probably thought that I'd just left work myself and was shopping before going home. If I'd told her there and then that I was off work until my guide dog came into my life, I have a feeling she may have stopped her judgemental chat. Finishing work 17 months previously had not been an easy option at all, but it was the only option at that time. I wondered whether I'd bump into the same lady when my guide dog arrived. She made me thankful that night that my life so far had made me appreciate people on a level that ran deeper than their occupation or status.

The next couple of days went past in a blur as my family helped me get the house ready for my new guide dog. It had been around 25 years since we'd had a dog in the family, so I searched my memory banks to recall what a dog would need. With frantic doggy-focused shopping trips done, I waited for him apprehensively yet patiently.

From the moment that I set eyes on him, I was in luuurrrvvveee – my 'I'm not really a dog person' belief chewed up and spat out within moments. When a blur the size of a miniature pony strutted in, dragging the trainer with him, my heart exploded with joy at his uniqueness. This big blur had the most powerful yet serene energy about him, and I knew he was my matching odd sock. He sniffed around for a good 20 minutes then came to sit by my feet for a fuss so we could meet each other properly. I began to connect with him, feeling that love that dog people must feel for their pets. I knew, too, that he would be a magnet for love from everyone he met.

He was not the usual Labrador, Golden Retriever or German Shepherd, but a large grey Labradoodle with distinguishing lighter grey around his face that made him look like he'd been around far longer than his tender 22 months on this Earth. To me, he looked like an old, wise dog with the face of a sage, the body of a warrior and the spirit of a guardian angel. His trainer told me she was often stopped in the street by people commenting that he looked older than his age, and saying, 'Isn't he getting on a bit to be a guide dog?' She was also quizzed if he really was a working guide dog, because he looked so different.

I think the universe had been in cahoots with our souls to bring our little alien worlds together at a time that was perfect for us both. When I put in the application form for my dog, albeit through gritted teeth, I never thought that I'd be able to connect so deeply with a furry friend. And yet, growing up with the blessing of feeling like an outsider meant I could welcome my fellow outsider with an open heart: he was one of my kind.

As the chat with the trainer went on I pretended to listen, yet my full attention was really on my new friend. It was clear from the start that his personality was as big as his stature, and I knew that I'd have my hands full with him. I've always been attracted to rebellious people and those who cause a little mischief: the naughty but nice. I knew straight away that he was one of those.

His name was Minster, as he was generously sponsored and named by Lincoln Minster prep school. Now Minster is such an official-sounding name, I'd expect it only of the most elite of dogs. Looking at him, I saw that he certainly had a regality about him, as the poodle in him really shone through. There was, however, another side to him that became obvious within minutes of meeting him. As he was not even two yet, his playfulness and mischievous manner mesmerized me in such a hypnotic way that it made it very hard to listen to the trainer. I could tell that his trainer, who had had him for the last few weeks, loved him dearly. She really understood his personality and accepted him for who he was. She affectionately referred to him as Munch, and this seemed a more fitting name when he was off-duty. We joked that Munch was so descriptive of him – not only because he munched everything in sight (that was the Labrador in him), but also because it gave rise to other nicknames like 'Monster Munch' and 'Munchkin', to name but a few.

After a bit more fuss and sniffing everything possible, Munch flopped on the floor and had a little snooze. It was only at this point that I really began paying attention to what his trainer was saying. We began talking about training and how the rest of the process would go from that day until I was fully qualified to have him. It all felt so real now. I was lucky that I was to train with Munch at home, as usually potential owners must travel to a hotel, which is about 60 miles away from my home. That would have been a little difficult with three children still living at home and a nine-month-old granddaughter whom I regularly looked after, so when I knew the training would be at home I felt so relieved. One of my sons is also autistic, so going away would have caused a lot of upheaval as a change in routine would have been a lot for him to cope with. It was enough change that we were going to have a dog. For several years I'd said no to having a pug, so having another dog now was potentially confusing and contradictory for him. Luckily, in the end he understood why I needed a guide dog that would be a little bigger than a pug.

As the trainer finished outlining what the rest of the three weeks' training would entail, I began picturing how this would be. I knew from that moment onwards that our Minster, or Munch as I'd call him off-duty, would fit into everyone's life as if he'd always belonged. To the outside world he would suit our madhouse quite well. I've brought my children up to be individuals and to think and act in keeping with their soul joy, so Munch would certainly blend into our family. There was, however, more to this sense of his belonging.

As we sat together, I knew that we understood each other at such a deep soul level. We mirrored each other so much. What really struck me was his peaceful presence, which I'd never before experienced in another being. It was like being before an Ascended Master, a teacher who has been through many lifetimes here on Earth and evolved into this all-knowing being. He flipped from playful pup to this wise old soul in a nanosecond and I saw his authentic soul in each of these roles. I really connected with his peace and authenticity. It was that place that many never reach in life, a place that many people work long and hard for, yet here we were, together and at peace with life in such a natural manner.

Peace is a place I've always known, where the true meaning of life resides. The place that consists of gratitude for life itself where everything else is a bonus. A place that no matter how bad life gets, there's always the knowledge that if you're alive and experiencing anything, even pain, then that's a blessing. Living in this magical place may sound cheesy or too good to be true, but that has been a natural state of being for me from birth. I knew that Munch was a permanent resident here, too.

When you live with a medical condition that can be fatal, it's almost impossible to feel blasé about life. As a small child I began entering this magical place of living when I felt detached from a world that made no sense to me. I never really understood what people with sight were talking about but here, in this realm of life, I knew there was more to living than what they spoke of. A sense of stillness would embrace me when others chose to argue and fight. It felt like a vortex into a world with no hostility, only acceptance. I slipped more into this world after I was diagnosed with Marfan syndrome and multiple tests began, from cardiology to orthopaedics and many stops in between. Nothing makes you delve more deeply into an alternative reality than an acute sense of difference.

With medical terms flying around me at such a young age and talk of future surgeries, it felt like I'd found a new partner in my failing eyesight. I realized that my sight loss was due to the alien invasion of Marfan syndrome in my body, but in a weird way, they worked well together. It felt like they complemented each other and it was up to me how I was going to host them. I had a choice to resent or love this condition that had been omnipresent from conception and would stay with me until my last day. I spoke to no one about my Marfan syndrome, nor about my sight loss. Even at such a young age I was aware that although I lived with a major condition, it was also irrelevant to who I was. This was the reason I chose to love my difference.

Living with recurrent pain and fatigue, I never once felt sorry for myself. Sprains, strains, broken bones and dislocations made me a regular at the accident and emergency department, but that was just life. When at eight years old I dislocated my jaw, I remember thinking I'd reached a new pain threshold and had to find a way to use my mind to take me to a place where pain did not exist. At that age I didn't know about meditation, but on reflection I now know that I used breathing and visualization techniques to take me to a place of meditative calm. I set goals to help me get through each day because I never wanted painkillers.

For a while, I was only able to eat a soft diet. On a family day out in Blackpool, slowly eating a soft strawberry and vanilla ice cream that my father had insisted on (I could not eat what the rest of the family was having). I recall thinking, *Life can't get any better than this*. I used the power of thought to transcend the pain and choose bliss. To this day,

I remember thinking that all this pain was worth it because I appreciated every mouthful I ate. I figured that transcending pain was easy when you just used your mind, and wondered why everyone didn't do this.

I learned to love the power of my mind and my stubbornness not to give in. My secret battle to overcome my health adversities meant I felt in control of my life. With a lowered immune system that upset all the connective tissue in my body in turn, even when ill I'd sweet-talk my body into a speedy recovery by promising it gifts. I bargained if I got better quickly, I'd treat it better in the future. I began witnessing pain and illnesses that happened in my body but chose not to give the pain energy. I knew even at a young age that my body did not represent me and who I was; it was there as a tool to help make my thoughts become reality.

Living with such a secret meant that it felt like I had to keep my positivity hidden, too, as nobody else seemed to have this attitude. Admitting to someone that I've never experienced deep grief sounds like I live in cloud-cuckoo-land. When a loved one passes away I see it as a blessing for them because I can literally feel their release from suffering. When I was nine years old, my grandfather died. He'd left his physical body but I knew that was not where he lived: his body was just a shell. He was Irish and I knew that he would be celebrating with everyone at his wake. This idea did not come from my parents or anyone around me; I just knew deep down that I had to truly live in my body. The one time that I shared my views on death with friends they told me I was weird to think like that, so I chose to not speak about it for years. I did not want the wedge I felt between me and others to grow even more, so I learned to keep my thoughts to myself.

When the word 'hate' was thrown around at school, I never quite got what was meant. I knew the feeling of anger and was okay at expressing it, dealing with it and letting it go. Hate, however, I never really understood, regardless of how many times other children gave me reasons for hating another person. If someone had been nasty, I understood that their behaviour was bad, but that wasn't who they really were – so how could you hate a fleeting moment? I knew of people who were nasty most of the time, but I never understood what that feeling of hate was, even when people spoke of the horrible things that they'd done. To this day, I still do not know what hate feels like. To me, life's truth is peace and love, so how can anything else exist? I feel anger when there's wrong-doing, but I counteract this with positive actions. I understand disappointment in a person or a situation, but that does not justify hate. I could always see the good in the most damaged of people, and still do.

Resilience is one of the best gifts of living with Marfan syndrome and sight loss. According to a Stress Inventory Rating Scale I should have become stressed out a long time ago, yet I can honestly say that I've never felt stressed. Divorce, moving to a new house, ill-health, losing a job and all the other things that may cause stress in an individual have always left me feeling inspired by new challenges. Of course I've felt sadness, but I've never been able to dwell in these negative thoughts, no matter how hard I tried. The worst part of living this way, though, is that it's so difficult to vocalize positive feelings in a world that seems so full of negativity. Here I was, having felt at peace with life from birth, while others spent years on self-development or pilgrimages to find that peace. This only added to my feeling of difference in the outside world. Connecting with like-minded people was a rarity.

This optimistic bubble I lived in was such a serene place and I knew that if I left it, it would be hard to return. Bad things happened in life, but I understood that they were happening for a reason. My logical mind would work alongside my emotions to help in hard times, but things always remained on a positive track. I learned to let the frustration go as I soon realized that people didn't feel as I did: there was always more to talk about with negativity than positivity. I craved an out-of-the-box thinker like me with whom I could share this love of the world. I did meet a few along the way who connected with certain ideas and belief systems I had, but not all. I truly accepted people's differences, but it usually felt one-sided.

I was so lucky to have such an amazing family who really did allow individuality to blossom. My parents operated a 'free parenting' kind of home, where they never tried to shape or mould us and just accepted us for who we were. Being of Welsh–Irish descent, a loving close family unit was a given and, although they were always supportive, they gave us freedom of choice. With both parents, my eldest brother and me all being born under the sign of Aries, independence was a strength we all shared and admired in one another. This at least was an advantage in shaping me into the resilient, grateful child that I became. They were the best role models a child could wish for when it came to altruistic behaviour, always helping others in selfless, caring ways, which allowed the optimism I saw in the world to be nurtured and encouraged. I only wished I could find more people like my family with whom to share my views on the world, but these odd socks were hard to find.

That was true until I met Munch. As soon as I met him I knew that he was of like mind – I could feel that off him straight away. I'd had different pets over the years and saw animals as equals, but I'd never met one like Munch. I knew that the Labradoodle has such a loving, placid temperament, yet his went beyond being a characteristic of his breed. It was also more than just his personality and early training. He had this aura about him that would calm the uncontrollable and bring out love in the most troubled souls. I could never have known, however, how life-changing he would be for so many people in such a short space of time.

As we sat together in the living room with the trainer, I knew that this odd sock knew exactly what it was like to live in the world wholly. We both had a mischievous side to us that loved life and this other side that knew, no matter what, that everything was always going to be okay.

CHAPTER 5

Munch Works in Mysterious Ways

Living our life purpose is so much easier when we know what our life purpose is. It's also true that when we identify what our life purpose is *not*, we can let go of what's unimportant and create space for our life purpose to develop. When we find out what motivates us and what crushes us and everything in between, we can begin to shape our lives in a more fulfilling way. Living a life that makes us happy just to 'be' is far simpler than our complex minds would have us believe.

Discovering what we were put on this Earth to do is not solely a human quest, as life in any form needs a reason to continue. All living things contain specialized, organized parts that allow them to exist physically. In psychological terms, the idea of life purpose differs greatly in every being – but there are similarities: each responds to stimuli, and grows, develops and evolves.

It's fair to say that Munch's life purpose depends upon who is being asked. If a non-dog lover was asked the purpose of Munch, maybe they would reply that his purpose is just to be a dog. Ask a dog lover and they will say he is here to keep us humans company. Ask a guide-dog representative and they may say that he is here to give back independence to a person with sight loss. I'd say he is here for all the above reasons and many more besides. Ask Munch himself, and the answers would be ones that we humans may never truly understand.

Munch (officially Minster) was born on 18 December 2014 to a Canadian-born, white male poodle named Pringle and a black Labrador mother, Hetty. He was one of 10 pups born to this loving pair who had been chosen to breed due to their placid and intelligent nature. Many of their pups have gone on to become qualified guide dogs, which shows that their pairing works well. When Munch was taken from his parents at seven weeks to be placed with his first puppy walkers, he really landed on his paws. He began his love of exploration as he was taken around different places where most dogs wouldn't be allowed. His inquisitive mind was stimulated by garden centres, shops, hairdressers, schools and vast open spaces, which became his paradise.

As he grew up into the ball of mischief that came racing through my door, he left his trail of magic on the people he met. His puppy walkers told of how he was known as the scruffy one in the village, and that people were always asking about him after he left them. He was well known at the local supermarket too, and the staff missed him when he left to become fully qualified. At one point during his training he was even a demonstration dog, although to be honest, everyone who knows him struggles to work out exactly what he was meant to be demonstrating. Maybe how to use your looks and charm to get out of working?

I was given his diary when he came to me at the young age of 22 months. As the narrator on my laptop read it out to me, it became clear that Munch was a natural-born entertainer and, although his work was to train as a guide dog, he had a far greater purpose in life than this. I know that all dogs have their own characters, which is so beautiful to witness, and it's these unique quirks that trigger emotions in us humans in the most powerful of ways. From birth, Munch has tended to do his own thing in his own way and if it involved any type of mischief, all the better.

As he visited Lincoln Minster prep school to meet the kind souls who sponsored him, he brought his cuteness out in full force to thank them for their generosity. Without their kind sponsorship, he wouldn't have been able to go through the expensive training and be able to give me back such independence. I will be forever grateful for the kindness that such young children and their families showed for a person whom they may never have met. Such acts highlight the amazing world we live in, where strangers help one another in the most altruistic ways.

Munch's poodle-like stubborn streak was one thing that I knew had been present from birth, and it challenged those who trained him. Doing things in his own way seems to have been a theme in his early puppy life, yet this gets left behind as soon as he puts on his harness and transforms from off-duty Munch to on-duty Minster. What he shows to the outside world is this amazingly well-trained dog who obeys commands, guides with grace and shows off his months of training. Not all dogs qualify and pass their training – some get withdrawn from service and are rehomed with loving families – so Munch's intelligence and commitment got him through this challenging time. Those who do make it through training work from around age two up until age nine, when they retire, so these dogs lovingly dedicate the best part of their lives to help us humans. The work they do is amazing, but it goes far beyond what the public sees. They become the missing piece of you.

When in 'Minster mode', he takes me to places that I'd never be able to go without him. He sees the obstacles that I might otherwise trip over. He becomes the reason people try to avoid bumping into us, as they see him coming along. He becomes the visual cue to a stranger that I may need a little assistance as I can't see. He changes our route if he sees roadworks blocking the pavement and figures out which way the barriers are taking us on an unfamiliar route. By wearing his harness, he is getting us permission to enter places that most dogs are not allowed. His physical roles while out working are numerous, but it does not stop here.

As he stops to meet friends old and new while out and about, he has a way of making a lasting impression, although not always for the right reasons. It seems that part of his role as a guide dog is to break the norm of what people expect to see in a guide-dog harness. His scruffy face and coat look like they belong on another breed of dog that wouldn't usually be with a blind person, which makes people stop and think how they judge others. By being the one who stands out from norm, he is the much-needed change in a world full of sameness. Many Labradoodles and other breeds are now being trained as guide dogs due to their characteristics and strengths. The reason he was chosen to be a guide dog, however, goes way beyond his physical talents.

I've learned to add extra time for our shopping trips so he can seek out people who need a friendly face, strategically placing himself under a lonely hand. As he becomes distracted from his role momentarily by sensing someone in need, he will gently side-step our planned destination and go and give someone some much-needed love. This could really throw the majority of guide-dog owners off balance and make their journeys harder – but it works for us. He would never cross a road we did not need to cross or lead me into danger, but he will always try his luck, helping me and another person at the same time, which is perfect.

One day when we were out I felt him pull me slightly over to the left, where I heard a toddler scream with excitement. We came to a sudden stop and I heard the little child cooing over him. Seconds later, I heard a frantic mother run right up to us, calling the child's name. The mother thanked us for stopping her child from running out into the road. I had no idea what she was talking about. Apparently her child had dropped a ball, which was heading for the road with her running after it. If off-duty Munch saw a ball bouncing freely around, he wouldn't hesitate to go straight into his 'ball thief' mode, but when he is in harness he avoids the urge and carries on with his duties. When he saw this child drop her ball and run after it, he quickened his pace and stopped in front of her because he could sense she was heading off the pavement and into the road. An onlooker told me this, describing how Munch had stood in front of the child, who was of similar height to him, so that she couldn't get past him into the road. This was not part of his training, but it came from his inbuilt desire to avoid any harm to anyone at all costs.

When I am working, he has sat in with me in counselling sessions with suicidal clients and not left their side until there's a break of hope in their saddened voices. With his floppy-eared head resting firmly on their laps, he does not move until they know that they're loved by this sloppy stranger. As he demands their attention I know that he's secretly coaxing them out from a lonely existence and reminding them what it can be like to reconnect with others with no questions asked. When they're seen as perfect through the non-judgemental eyes of an animal, living instead of existing becomes a possibility. As he befriends the bullied, he helps them remember that they're never to blame for other people's faulty thinking. At the same time each week, he waits patiently behind the counselling room door to welcome them with open paws and to be the much-needed peace in a world full of hostility. He has become the constant in an ever-changing world for many.

His off-duty Munch persona is the one I love so much, and I never tire of his mischievous ways. Even when he is in Minster mode, his Munch side always shines through but may not be picked up by the untrained eye. His sage-like ways are a saving grace for him from getting into trouble, as I'd feel bad giving such a knowledgeable old soul a row for doing doggy things. He allows me to re-evaluate what is important in life and what is insignificant. As he races around the house with my bra flopping in sync with his ears, I am reminded of the fact that possessions can never be as valuable as quality time spent with him. As he ups the mischief stakes weekly, he brings my attention to his need to feel appreciated. Dog behaviourists may have a meltdown about him running off with anything he shouldn't have, but I know it's my cue to get off the laptop and have a break with him.

Everyone needs a reminder now and again to spend more time doing what really matters in this world, so I thank him every time.

From reading his diary from when he was a pup, I found out that I'd handed my notice in at work on his first birthday. With such synchronized timing, it was inevitable that our partnership would work well together. A year and half earlier I'd sat with a good friend of mine at a local park and told her I was thinking of applying for a guide dog, but was doing so with resentment. Being independent for all these years meant that I'd lived with a severe visual impairment with only a few knowing and was still able to continue, 'aid'-free. We joked that my stubbornness was taking a knock and that it had better be a very special dog to come into my life to make me feel okay with showing this side of myself to others. As we spoke I could not imagine being given a golden Labrador, as that would be too normal. Little did I know that our little Munch was being conceived around that time, so it felt like the universe had heard my wish and was getting ready to create a masterpiece of mystery.

When Munch was going through his intense training, I was beginning to feel deskilled because I'd given up work. As he explored more of the world that he was being introduced to, my world was getting smaller and smaller as I'd stopped going out alone. It was as if the universe was balancing out our lives by creating extremes at that exact moment in time. The beauty in this balancing act meant that when we finally met, our past experiences merged into a solid foundation for our future partnership.

As I sit and merge into his mystery, it's apparent that he is here not just for my benefit, but for the benefit of others, too. Not that he is here solely to be of service to others, but as he benefits others, he also benefits tenfold back. He triggers an exchange not only of attention, but he also offers a deep sense of connection. The love of an animal has a way of taking us back to basics, making us stop to remember the importance of others. Anyone can choose to live apart from society if they so wish, but living such a life can bring more harm than good. If we're left with just ourselves, we can forget that we're just as important as the next person. If we forget the kindness of others, we can forget to be kind to ourselves. The same is true in reverse, as if we think only of ourselves and forget to be kind to others, our lives can feel like they revolve around us – which may make the ego happy, but it will also make the heart lonely. By sharing moments with another being, whether human or non-human, we learn to step outside our own lives and into the lives of others.

Caring for animals is one of the first ways children begin to understand the importance of others. I remember when my beautiful granddaughter met Munch when she was nine months old. The sharing began as a game that many babies enjoy, with her dropping food from her highchair into the eager mouth of Munch, who would magically appear underneath. With Munch an ever-ready participant in this new-found game, the bond between child and dog deepened. Despite our determination to stop Munch from joining in, my granddaughter's determination was stronger and their relationship, based on food appreciation, left the highchair and spread into other parts of life. When she sleeps over, Munch is the first one she checks on in the morning when she wakes. She throws a ball for him and does anything she can to entertain her furry friend. Through being around him, she has learned the importance of sharing whatever she can with him. This is so heartening to see, because she is showing that she understands that the needs of others are equal to her own – a concept that will get her through life.

When Munch and I go and work in schools or speak to groups of people in the community about the important work of guide dogs, he is also educating people about what sight loss is and is not. I answer curious questions about him, like 'Can he read signs?' or 'Does he go to human toilets?' and other out-of-the-box musings, bringing knowledge to enquiring minds along with an awareness that everyone's needs are different. Being kind and thoughtful may be something we naturally expect from others, but this is not always the case. As we have slipped into a world that promotes our self-importance as a paramount standard, we can sometimes forget the concept that other people are just as important as ourselves. Understanding how other people live can therefore help us feel more connected to people who we may not normally spend time with.

Munch weaves his magic and mystery into the lives of people in almost covert ways. The encounters we have with anything from a flower to a human have a personal meaning for us that others may not get; a meaning that can never come from an outside source, only from within. When we meet other people, we can feel like we're the only ones in that situation with feelings – or, alternatively, sense that the other person's feelings are more important than our own. Overall, our approach is to know that each one of us has equally important feelings. By taking this knowing as a rule for life, we open up to a more serene way of living. Being as kind to others as we are to ourselves allows us to return to the basics of humanity.

Observing animal behaviour and how animals interact with humans never fails to teach us things we may have forgotten. Dogs thrive on the basics of life, with food, play and fuss being the main highlights of their lives. They choose how they want to react and take the lead in owning their choices. All living beings have a choice to accept or reject what they're faced with; this is an omnipresent law of the universe. A whole species can't act in the same way, so believing that we're programmed to act or feel in a specific way can't be right, otherwise there would be no variation in a species. Finding what is unique in us and in all living beings allows us to break through restrictions and see the world in a different light.

The behaviour that Munch displays a lot of the time can only be described as more human than canine. From sighs of impatience to requiring a pillow for his head, he loves to feel like part of the family. I know that his behaviour is learned through imitating the many people who have been part of his life, but it seems to be much more than that. The old-soul energy he brings to this world goes far deeper than I will ever know. The more I accept him and his quirky ways, the more he seems to show his authentic self. His placid outlook on life allows him to observe the world. He lives in his own serene bubble, which matches my identical bubble perfectly. His stimulus in life appears to be the cessation of any involvement in drama that does not serve him. As he witnesses the world go by, he chooses what to give attention to and what to ignore.

His growth has not just been in physical terms, turning from a black bundle of hair at birth into the body of a small pony, but he has also learned the art of tolerance. Working with someone with sight loss must be quite a difficult task for a guide dog, as they're constantly using their senses to keep us safe and out of danger. They put their own needs on hold and put ours first, which is such a compassionate thing for them to do. Their instinct to play, eat or pee on things that they see out and about gets ignored as they revert to the discipline of their training. Even on days when he would rather lounge around on the sofa or on one of our beds, he gets up and goes to work for minimal reward in physical terms. When I hesitate in new places that I'm unsure of, he just calmly takes over and finds an alternative route to take us through. He never loses his patience as a human would. He just gently plods along on his life path, with me following gratefully behind.

Evolving through our own lifetime means we must go through stages and phases to be able to reach our full potential. It may be slightly different for dogs, who do not feel that fulfilling their life purpose depends on becoming prime minister, but they do have their own version. There are obvious ways in which a dog naturally evolves from playful pup to serious old senior. It also takes a lot of unlearning for them to go from their old puppy behaviour to grown-up behaviour. Munch, now nearly four, still has a lot of puppy-like behaviours left in him and I have a feeling that they will always be there. The nosy nature of a Labradoodle may always lead him into mischief, but that's just part of his charm. Since he has come to me, we have learned to adapt to each other's way of life and evolve together in a world that has changed for both of us. I feel that I've had the best of the bargain, though, as he gives me much more than I ever feel I can give him. Unconditional love, attention, playtime and treating him as an equal does not seem a fraction of the repayment he deserves for changing my life in breath-taking ways. I don't think there's any way he could further evolve into a better being.

Having such a positive influence around me has made me want to strive to be a better person. While it was never a conscious decision to keep Marfan syndrome and sight loss hidden from the world, nor had I wanted to wear it on my sleeve. It has never really bothered me; it just 'is', as I've known no different. And I thought that I could not think of it in a different way. That was until I remembered my golden rule – the rule that says the world is not about me, it's about *us*. In every area of my life I've always sought out equality and viewed everyone as the same, regardless of our differences. After meeting Munch, I was forced to stop and think about how equal I felt to other people with sight loss if I did not see myself as sharing similarities with them. The universe pairing me up with such a unique dog meant that people would begin to see me and ask questions, so it was about time I got ready to answer them.

What I didn't know then was that the universe was having a good laugh at us behind our backs as it had picked the biggest pair of synced-up souls that may ever have inhabited this Earth. Instead of my fretting about what people would think of my new best friend, I should have felt relaxed in the knowledge that what I had done, he had done and what I would do, he would do. Minus the peeing against lamp posts and sniffing people's bums, we have a very similar approach to being in society. Our attitude to life is relatively simple: live and let live. The only thing that complicated our lives was that we sometimes forgot that we lived in bodies. It took some very awkward events to help us return from our daydream world to the physical reality of our existence.

It was so lovely having a clumsy partner join me in life after feeling so different for so long.

CHAPTER 6

The Clumsy Patchwork Quilts

Our life's themes, like patches on a multicoloured quilt, are never the same as the next person's; some of our quilts have patches of excitement and adventure, whereas others show a little more serenity. When my quilt met Munch's, it was clear to see we shared lots of the same patches. Many were positive and showed strength; then there were the others – notably, the patches that signified 'clumsy'. I soon discovered that the 'clumsy patches' in my quilt ran alongside Munch's in perfect sync.

Growing up, clumsiness had always been my loyal companion. It never strayed far from me in my daily life. Part of the reason that clumsiness remained so dedicated to me was due to the simple fact that I could not see. Another reason was that I often forgot (and still do) that I live in a human body. This is a common problem for those of us who have imagination and are thought addicts, so busy thinking, planning and daydreaming that we forget we can control our own bodies (this is my excuse, anyway, when people see me in a post-mishap pose). While I was not born with elegance or normality, I was certainly born with cringe-worthy comic timing.

Many years ago, before I met Munch, my then partner and I decided to go to Oakwood Theme Park in Pembrokeshire, Wales, for the day for a bit of an adrenaline fix. Waiting in the queue to go on the rollercoaster, I tried to figure out where the rollercoaster would pull up to let the previous petrified lot off and let us eager excited lot on. As blurry bodies left the carriages, I thought I'd lead the way to our awaiting seats. Well, I thought they were seats. I climbed aboard part of the carriage that seemed a lot higher than the other blurs and attempted to sit down. As I slid my bum along the weirdest-feeling seat that I'd ever felt, my partner called out, 'Zena! What are you doing?' and told me I was sitting on top of the carriage instead of inside it. As I hastily got off, trying to hide my embarrassment, the theme-park worker in charge of the rollercoaster came over and said, 'Oh, you've decided to join the others in the normal seating arrangement, then?' Just to clarify, this was when my eyesight was at its best. For some strange reason this has put me off rollercoasters ever since.

Seating arrangements tend to baffle Munch, too. Not only because he thinks he's trapped in a chihuahua's body, but because he also seems to have 'harness-only' depth perception. When he slips on his harness and becomes professional Minster, he can assess distances with immense precision. As he guides me, he can naturally judge if we will be able to fit through a small gap between a wall and a car parked on the pavement. As he looks ahead he can tell if an overhanging object at face height will hit me and if so, he will stop, look back and refuse to let me go further. Then he'll find a safer route. He is amazing at his job, but when he's off-duty this impeccable judgement disappears. He falls off sofas, beds and any object not at floor level. He once tried to sit down in a basket too small for him and somehow got his bum wedged snugly in it. Once, he tried to sit on the slope of a hill and roly-polied down at quite a speed. As he gets up from these calamities, he casually walks away like it was meant to have happened. I certainly know that feeling.

If there were an Olympic competition for clumsiness, we would be the duo to beat. Within the first few seconds of meeting Munch I thought he belonged to the elegant and somewhat normal race that inhabits the Earth, but I exhaled a sigh of relief when I found out he was one of my clumsy lot. He may look like a gliding, graceful god when he makes an entrance, but observe him long enough and you will discover his ungainly blunders. He sometimes acts in such a lovable, dippy way that you can't help but fall more deeply in love with him.

My clumsiness has been on top form many times and I can sometimes score a hat-trick in one day or night. Back when I was at university, student nights out were always on offer. With two small children to look after I didn't go to many, but when I did, I tended to make an impact. One night, my cocktail of clumsiness overflowed. Always one of the first to dance, I thought that dancing on the stage seemed such a good idea, but it didn't take long for me to realize otherwise. While dancing on a dark stage on a dark floor in a darkened room is never ideal, it's a little more challenging with a visual impairment. The bright lights became my new-found friends as they shone on people around me, so I could kind of guess where these blurs were dancing and stay away to avoid bumping into them. As I danced away embracing the music in my own bubble, I thought I'd invented a new move as I fluttered through the air and felt a multitude of hands all over my body. It was only when the floor came up to meet me after this new-found dance move that I realized I'd fallen off the stage. Luckily, my blushes were hidden from the bodies of the people attached to the outstretched hands giving me back the contents of my bag.

Not one to leave the laugh-filled onlookers in suspense, I didn't make them wait too long before my next blunder of the night. To soothe my ego into submission, I promised it some alcohol. I'd been drinking soft drinks up until then, but I thought some alcohol may persuade my bruised ego into talking to me again, so I went with my friends to get a drink. Chatting away, we decided to try to find a seat. There were none available, so we loitered with intent near some tables and chairs that were apparently there and waited for people to leave. As I finished my drink I wondered where I might put my glass. My friend told me where to find an empty table, so off I went in what I thought was the right direction. All I could see was a pair of white legs flopped either side of a table (at least, that's what my mind told me). This same conniving brain told me that the positioning of the flopped legs either side meant that there was a table in between these legs, and that this was the table my friend had described. As I lowered my empty glass onto this imaginary table, I saw the white legs growing closer together until they became a unified white line. It was only as my glass gently touched down on the crotch of a poor terrified man that I realized there was no table and he'd just been sitting with his legs akimbo. The panicky apology that I shouted at him over the blaring music felt a little too late. And I really hoped that the CCTV cameras were not working that night.

Reassuring my still-laughing friends that I was safe to be left without adult supervision, I went to find the toilet (I'd been to this venue before, so I wasn't unduly worried about finding my way). En route, I pulled out my phone to text my partner to give him a good chuckle about my escapades that night. As I was busy holding my phone close to my face to attempt to text, I miscounted the doors and ended up going into the door marked 'staff only', which led behind the bar. As I was so engrossed in texting, I just pushed the door open with my arms and did not bother looking up to see where I was. It was only when my feet started sliding forwards at a rapid pace that I thought it may be a good idea to find something to grab on to. The nearest object was a pair of hairy arms holding a mop, which I ended up nose-butting and hugging at the same time. As I looked around I realized I'd slipped on a spillage on the floor behind the bar and was confronted by a very confused-looking man. This really was a hat-trick night.

It's nice to know now that my furry soul mate Munch also has this hat-trick ability, so I can feel more relaxed in the knowledge that I am not the only clown around. One of his hat-trick days came while we were staying in a hotel overnight for a workshop. I'd taken a ball and some toys for him to play with while he was off-duty so that he could relax and enjoy himself. What I hadn't thought about was his innate ability to bump into things and get stuck in places that many would never dream of going. Within a short space of time, Munch managed to get stuck under the bed three times. He dove under the bed at record speed, yet could not work out how to reverse.

On each of these occasions I had to lift the bed while he slowly reversed back into the room. I thought after the first time he may have learned his lesson, but apparently not. The second time he seemed to think it would be appropriate to take longer to get out as I struggled to hold up the bed in mid-air. The third time he got stuck I swear I heard him laugh, as he knew his lowly maid had yet again to lift the bed for him. He even stopped for a downward facing dog yoga pose and had a lovely stretch before he removed his whole body from under there. With hindsight, any normal person would have stopped throwing the ball to prevent him having to perform this muscle-aching manoeuvre to get him out, but oh no, I had to be the last to catch on to common sense.

We have grown so close since meeting one another. As any animal lover knows, pets love to feel close to their owners and follow them everywhere, even into the bathroom. This no-privacy rule has its advantages – as a guide-dog owner you have no real choice but to take them with you into the toilet when you're out and about. For the first few months with Munch I avoided using the disabled toilets as I felt like I wasn't disabled. While out shopping one day I needed the toilet, so we headed for the ladies. I tried to reassure my analytical brain that there was enough room in the cubicle for both me and my Shetland pony-sized dog. On this occasion, like many other times, I was wrong.

Munch went into the narrow cubicle first, so I tried to push past him, but I misjudged the size of the cubicle and realized we both wouldn't get in. Ever the optimist, I was determined to make this work, so I stepped carefully over him. To make things easier I hovered my foot above the toilet, pirouetting on my other leg to close the door. My un-ballerina-like body had other ideas and my hovering foot made the biggest plop ever as it landed at a funny angle in the toilet bowl. On the plus side, Munch managed to close the door with his nose, so the original plan had kind of worked. As he turned his back on me and sighed loudly, I swear he was rolling his eyes, too. I was now left trying to figure out how to get my foot out of the toilet. I had not long come out of a full leg-cast after dislocating my knee and causing soft tissue damage for the umpteenth time, so I knew I could not just pull it out, as I really didn't fancy doing more damage not only to my knee, but also to a paramedic's state of mind should I need to call for help. After managing to balance on the cistern of the toilet with my other leg, I gently persuaded my submerged foot to come out, with a promise to disinfect it when I got home.

Mirroring each other's blunders has become common practice for Munch and me. I secretly think the universe has an ongoing bet to see if we'll score even or if one of us will outdo the other. After this foot-down-the-bog incident, Munch decided to equal the score by getting his own feet caught in a bog.

When out free-running one day with a friend of mine, Munch decided he was going to try to break the speed of sound and run wildly along without a care in the world. Munch is one of those dogs usually nosing over his shoulder when out free-running, not bothering to look ahead. No matter how many times he bangs into a lamp post or trips over a gust of wind, he still hasn't learned to look where he's going. This day, he was running along a wooden walkway that ran parallel to a lake. He'd already been in the lake to have a swim and thought he would go for another, so he tried to jump into the inviting water. His half-hearted jump landed him in the boggy ground next to the lake. With his two front paws sunk deep into the boggy ground and his back two waiting patiently for him to rejoin the rest of his body, he began to panic. After my friend spent an exhausting few minutes trying to free him, his four paws were finally reunited. He seemed to slow down on the rest of his walk and take a little more care where he was going. This caution didn't last, though.

The clumsiness patch on my quilt appeared back in childhood due to too many incidents to recall, but a few do stand out. As depth perception has never been my strong point (the distance between blurs A and B looks pretty much standard to me), I knew I had to be cautious in certain situations. I remember a school disco in primary school. We were playing the old game of Oranges and Lemons in which a line of children goes underneath the outstretched arms of other children, forming an archway. Combining my innate clumsiness with subluxated lenses, which meant it took a while to focus, was a recipe for disaster. As I lined up with the rest of the children I was wondering how I'd know where the archway ended, as I could not see that far. As the line started moving with the onset of music, the first run through the archway of arms went well. It was on the third unlucky go that I realized my attempt to blend in with the fully sighted had failed. Seeing with my normal double vision, I charged forwards into a sea of body parts and kicked out of the way what I thought was a stray crisp packet on the rubbish-strewn floor. My ferocious kick hit my target, which I later found out was not a crisp packet but a foot. As our feet made a colossal impact, I lost balance and charged at the children on both sides of the arch in a tackle that any professional rugby player would be proud of. As I heard the children fall like dominoes, I felt so guilty. The silence was interrupted by screams and crying when the music stopped, and I wanted to disappear. I spent the rest of the night apologizing to the other children and vowed to treat apparent crisp packets with far more respect in the future.

It may just be the sight of an inviting archway that makes us clumsy people think that we can go through them like normal people without any fuss. After all, what could possibly go wrong? You just walk in a straight line and come out the other side, right? It seems that Munch has the same default mode as I do when it comes to something as simple as this. When he first came to us, I was assured it was normal doggy behaviour for him to give his doggy cuddles by passing through the open legs of us humans; it was their version of hugging. I thought it was so sweet and encouraged him to do it whenever he felt like it. As this became a common sign of affection for him with his loved ones, I never stopped to think whether this may or may not be socially acceptable.

Munch had come with me to my uncle's funeral. I was sat by my mother during the service and Munch, bless him, had been on his best behaviour – but he changed when he went outside afterwards, sensing a more relaxed atmosphere as we went to speak with those who had attended. He adores my mother and dived in head-first between her legs for his cuddle. The only problem was that my mother is only 4ft 11in with a 25-in inside leg, and Munch is a rather tall dog. Given his angle of approach and my mother's long skirt, now shortened and stretched over his body, my mother could not escape. So, after he'd finished his cuddle, he tried to move off but didn't realize that even with my mother balancing on tiptoe, escaping was a little difficult. Any onlookers would have seen the back of this petite lady's body with a dog sticking out between her legs – not the most common sight at a funeral. As Minster Munch tried to move away, he took my mother with him. As he trotted off, my mother resembled a backwards-facing jockey holding on for dear life. It was okay, though, as after we finished laughing we did manage to help her off by gently tipping her to one side. This hasn't put Munch off giving people cuddles in this way, though, and if anything, it has made him do it more.

The clumsy patches of our quilts, as you can see, are quite well matched. I think we tap into each other's psyches and up the stakes each time one of us has a moment or two of mishaps. Up until I met Munch, I always felt like the odd one out. It never really bothered me much as I knew my way of being in the world suited me. The great thing is when you live your life making multiple mistakes in front of eager witnesses, you're just being human. I'd much rather spend my time with real humans who feel okay with making mistakes, and would choose them over the perfect kind of people in life. Those are the ones who make me uneasy.

Our quilts are not only made up of the clumsy patches, though – we do have other parts, as does everyone. The most noticeable are the patches of uniqueness. Everyone has their own patch of uniqueness on their quilt, which makes them who they really are. It's here that the true self can be found, either on show for all to see or hidden away for all to miss. Our appearance to the outside world is rooted here, and feeling comfortable in our own skin is supported or declined in this place. Mine and Munch's unique patches represent not fitting in; being told that we do not look like a guide dog nor a 'blind owner'. We do not need to conform to labels to be happy.

If you have other misfits around you, life will never be dull. The great thing about feeling different from others is freedom; not having to fit in with the rules that everyone else follows. Doing your own thing your own way can be far more fun.

Another large patch that appears on both of our quilts is that of positivity. Watching Munch plod on in life regardless of what gets in his way is so refreshing. Whether he's getting snarled at by a little dog while working or being slightly jumpy around a passing lorry, he shakes it off and moves on. He observes things as they happen, yet never gets drawn in. He always has that get-up-and-go inherent in all optimists.

Positivity is innate in me. Even as a child I found it hard to find the negative in any situation. Things happened, but I knew they always happened for a reason. When others saw the negative in something I found it hard to understand what they meant but rarely voiced my opinions. Living with a time-bomb condition such as Marfan syndrome really makes you put your life into perspective. Fatality can be a reality with Marfan syndrome, so why cloud the reality of life with negative thoughts? From heart scans at age five, I knew that health should be respected and honoured, not taken for granted. While I am thankful to wake up each morning, when people moan at the slightest of things I really begin to wish I could live somewhere else. I know that life is far too precious to whittle away on whining, so I avoid it at all costs. Meeting Munch meant that I could share this positive outlook on the world without being criticized for living too much in the land of the unicorns.

Another patch that's mirrored in our quilts is acceptance. People vary greatly in this world, and this makes it such an amazing place in which to live. The flaw in one person can be the strength in another. Nobody is perfect, so why judge another? The beauty in being blind is that you can never take anyone at face value. We humans are such complex beings; the actions of an individual may be judged as bad, yet the reason for their actions lies within the network of neurons that lies within each of us. I feel that we were all born into this world as perfect beings, so returning to such perfection is never impossible if we choose to do so. Munch has an ability to home in on people most in need of loving acceptance. When he sits in my counselling room with a client in distress, he is there for them whole-heartedly, which they can sense when he gives them his doggy, slobbery kisses. I may not give slobbery kisses to everyone I meet, but I do accept them for who they are. Bad choices in life and less than desirable behaviour do not mean that a person is bad. I am far from perfect, so why would I expect so much from anyone else?

Everybody has their own patchwork quilt that evolves throughout life. Some patches can be removed or added as life goes on. People may think that the patches they're born with define who they really are, but this is not true; we're the masters of our lives. If you don't like something, change it. If you love something, feed it. Looking outside ourselves for support can be helpful, but real change must come from within. Changes can be scary, but the unknown can hold so much potential. A lot of people are afraid of creating their ideal life; success can seem too good to be true. They stay in their comfort zone because it seems a little safer. Yet, if we're too afraid to change any of the patches on our quilts, we will only get what we have always had. Changing your thoughts from negative ones to positive ones can have life-changing results, so why not try?

Themes that run through our lives exist because, at some level, we created them. Unless we change the way we act and feel about the world, there they will remain. When we realize that we're in control of how we feel, life gets a little easier. If you can't change a situation, change how you feel about the situation. It seems like so much hard work to see the negatives in life and moan about minor things, creating nothing but stress. When you get in touch with the feelings and themes of your quilt patches, you feed your passions and starve your fears.

The clumsiness that Munch and I share is fine with us. Other people experiencing the same calamities may react quite differently, but for us, it's okay. Being the charismatic Labradoodle that he is, the clumsiness running through his blood only adds to his appeal.

His 'daft dog' moments do amuse onlookers. Animals never take themselves too seriously, and I love that about them. They mess up, they get up and they carry on. They never worry who has seen them or stress needlessly about what other people think about them. They don't need to worry if their blunders end up going viral on YouTube. The simplicity of their lives can teach us what it can be like, living without fear of judgement.

We can own our feelings. We can own our thoughts. We can control our actions. We can control our lives. We can't control any of these in another person, so why waste energy trying to do so? If we wish to change for ourselves, then we should. If we wish to change for another, we should not. What we should do is become the best 'me' in life, regardless of our imperfections.

I've grown over the years not to care what others think of me and I accept the clumsy part of who I am. We all have different personalities, strengths and weaknesses, none of which will ever be perfect, but they're perfect for us. The ability to laugh at ourselves is essential. This is truer if you live with a disability or health condition, as the chances are you will be faced with certain obstacles that others may not understand or have experienced. Living in a body with limits does not mean that there should be a limit in our minds.

I often wonder what life would have been like had I been born with a perfectly healthy body. A body with a musculoskeletal system that matched everyone else's; a straight spine, not curved; fully functioning eyes that would let you see what beauty lies in nature, and in the most miniscule of detail. This body would work at a 'normal' rate, so multiple connective tissue systems wouldn't have to work extra hard on a day-to-day basis, and fatigue would be non-existent. In this fictional body, bones and joints stay strong and don't break or dislocate. Heart and lungs work in perfect harmony, never becoming a threat to life. Yet this fictional, fully working body that my mind creates wouldn't make me a happier person. Having never known ill-health, I don't think I'd appreciate it as much.

The hidden ability in disability can be such a beautiful quality to discover. This patch on the quilt of life holds so much potential for a person, yet they and those around them may be oblivious to it. Changing how we see disability and how we utilize its potential can greatly enhance a person's life. Disability is not an easy thing to live with, but for many, it can be empowering.

Often, it's the patchwork quilts of those with a disability or a health condition that are the most beautiful of all.

CHAPTER 7

More Abled Than Disabled

As the pen lingers a few inches above the medical form, we groan in unison at the dreaded questions: 'Any Disability?' and 'Any Epilepsy, Heart Conditions...?' Our dilemma: neither of these is technically applicable and we need another box. My daughter finds one – 'Any other information' – and writes down 'Marfan syndrome'. As we know, this will inevitably lead to more details being required at a future date. Declaring a connective tissue disorder that potentially affects such a range of bodily systems can be so frustrating.

My daughters Rasheena and Korisha had been helping me with forms for quite a few years. Any school consent forms, medical forms or such that needed filling in, they were my go-to angels. They could see the lines and spaces, whereas I just saw blurs, so they helped me to complete them and never once complained. Never complained, that is, until these questions came up. The catch-22 is that although Marfan syndrome itself is not classed as a disability, nor is it classed as good health. Words such as 'prone to' and 'at greater significant risk' were often thrown around, so we always had to declare our condition on all forms. We carried a card around with us saying that as a Marfan patient we were more at risk of aortic dissection (a tear in the heart's major artery), retinal detachment, joint dislocations, pneumothorax (collapsed lungs) and other scary-sounding stuff. Many of these risks are rare but can happen, so I spent many years researching reports and guidelines on what we should and should not do, and used this information to educate professionals in the children's lives when drawing up care plans in case of emergencies.

Marfan syndrome limits certain activities. Many contact sports are not recommended, along with diving, skydiving, lifting excessive weights and any other activities that could increase the likelihood of anything from a subluxated lens to an aortic dissection. The frustrating thing was, though, that these were more of a 'just in case' scenario rather than a known disability. From the complexity of the disorder, disabilities could arise. The lens subluxation and dodgy eye structure I'd been born with made me partially sighted from birth and now registered blind. Others with extreme hypermobility and joint issues develop into a disability on mobility grounds, yet there are many who suffer a multitude of differing connective tissue issues – and these people are not classed as disabled. It was far from straightforward.

As three out of four of my children have Marfan syndrome, we have spent the last 20 years in and out of outpatient departments. From ophthalmology to cardiology, paediatrics to orthopaedic departments, we have done our rounds. Accident and emergency departments have also been a favourite haunt of ours, especially for my accident-prone son, Zaidley – with broken bones, head injuries and 'just in case' checks. As soon as an accident happened in school, we were always phoned to get the children checked 'just in case'.

My two sons, Jaidan and Zaidley, were diagnosed when one was aged 17 months and the other three years old during an eye examination. My daughter was to wait until she was 18 to have genetic testing and receive her diagnosis, although many positive signs of the condition were apparent from birth. For a diagnosis of Marfan syndrome you must meet two of the stated criteria of family history, skeletal features, pulmonary involvement, cardiovascular involvement and ocular issues, such as lens subluxation. Despite her meeting three of these criteria, the medical professionals still held off from a diagnosis even though I could tell from birth that she had it. It was a relief for her when she finally had the diagnosis, as it confirmed what she'd been aware of from a young age. I'd always been honest when the children questioned me about why they had to attend the medical appointments and they knew what Marfan syndrome was. One of the most annoying things about disclosing such a complex medical condition was filling out those dreaded forms.

Under the Equality Act of 2010, you're disabled if 'You have a physical or mental impairment that has a "substantial" and "long-term" negative effect on your ability to do normal daily activities.' However, in day-to-day living, many conditions have periods of flare-up and other times when the individual can be physically okay for a lengthy period. Disorders of the immune system, for example, may be inactive or active at any given time, but the person still lives with it daily. So, conditions such as Marfan's may not technically be considered a disability because they do not necessarily exhibit all the potential symptoms all the time. As the Act's definition of disability is vague, the definition is arguably open to interpretation.

The Equality Act does, however, give a generic view that's officially accepted in both mental and physical health regarding disability. Acknowledging the mental as well as the physical health of an individual can have a positive impact and this wording has been warmly welcomed by those in the mental health field. In this sense, the Act has brought about positive change.

Over the years there has been a great push towards educating the public about what disability really is and highlighting hidden disabilities that should not be ignored. Although there's still more work to be done, the boundaries between disabled and non-disabled individuals have come a long way down over the last few decades.

Within disability itself, there's a split between how disabled individuals identify with or separate themselves from the 'disabled' label. Some people feel they've had to battle through life to get equal treatment and the same standard of living as able-bodied individuals. There are others who get on with their lives regardless of their disability, and don't allow themselves to become labelled by the outside world. The ones who don't fit into these groups may fluctuate between the two throughout their lives. It's complex: people identify with their disability in differing ways, and it's important to recognize the views of the individual. A person's relationship with their health can also affect whether their condition makes them feel depleted or empowered.

If Louis Braille had chosen to accept that he could not read or write, blind and partially sighted people may have remained isolated from the written word. If we come across something that does not exist, is it not our place to invent that something that's needed in the world by any means possible? Sign language as we know it today may never have been developed if Juan Pablo Bonet had waited around for someone else to publish a text for an alternative form of communication. If we can create something that will help people who you may never meet, why would you choose not to? If Stephen Hawking had feared motor neurone disease and focused on its limitations, he wouldn't have contributed so greatly to the world of science through his life-long dedication to research. Surely his label of disability would have been enough to halt his belief in himself, if he'd allowed it to. Temple Grandin, a leading American academic, chose to use the beauty of her autism to become an inspiring lead in the field of psychology and agriculture, and has helped to raise positive awareness towards disability. She used her amazing strengths to dispel the perceived weaknesses in other disabled individuals. Had Nick Vujicic been born with limbs, he may not have become one of the world's leading motivational speakers today, inspiring millions. Had he been born with limbs, which he may have taken for granted, would he be living his life as fully as he does today?

Without the Paralympics, we might still believe that great physical capabilities are only given to those who are historically healthy. Without models with Down syndrome and models who are amputees gracing the catwalk with their natural beauty, an archaic view of beauty would still exist. Such individuals would be left out of mainstream media and remain hidden. If campaigners had not fought a discriminatory system, equal opportunity legislation wouldn't exist today. Such people would have been silenced, continuing to feel deficient in comparison to others. Diversity is being driven into society for a reason. When we begin to understand that we're more than our bodies, we begin to enter the realm of equality, which is such a peaceful place to exist. Competition can't exist in a place where everyone is seen as whole and perfect just as they are.

The individuals mentioned previously demonstrate that even when faced with a disability, ability can grow in a seemingly futile place. As the definition of disability states, the impact of a disability on daily living can be significant, so how is it that some people turn this challenge into a positive for change? It's not disability alone that causes adverse circumstances in health; there are also many illnesses and conditions that have a major impact on quality of life, too. Intermittent health challenges that arise through life can affect anyone. Some may be fleeting, while others make themselves comfy for weeks, months or years before disappearing as quickly as they came. From cancers to colds, vertigo to bouts of mental illness, it's rare to go through life without any health hiccups one way or another.

A lack of adversity can be a barrier to finding your true life purpose; many people breeze through life without any hurdles, and never seem to discover their purpose. Then there are the 'Midas magicians' who use their adversity, choosing to find purpose where others see misery – one person's hardship can be another person's drive. The difference between suffering and living on purpose is down to the way we think. Inspirational people are not born with a magic wand; they develop a magical way of living through the way they choose to see the world. Living with a disability, health condition or in adverse circumstances can make you question life at a much deeper level. It's here, in the realm of questioning, that the meaning of life can be found.

Life becomes more precious when you know it can change in an instant. Finding your life purpose can come about in the strangest of ways, or it may remain hidden for years. Even in adversity there's beauty to be found by those who wish to look. There's no circumstance in life that's too big to be fought through to create the change you wish to see. Finding your own life purpose can be the greatest gift to yourself and to the world.

When we choose to see the positives in a seemingly dismal situation we're investing in our future wellbeing. When we choose to stop focusing on what doesn't work and look at what does work, we begin to realize that life is not so tough, after all. When we choose to use the weaknesses that others may see in us and turn them into strengths, we know there's nothing in this world that we can't beat. Choosing to remember that we're more than our physical or mental health may be a hard concept to grasp at first, but when it sinks in, it can begin to change how we live our life. When we choose to choose, we win at life.

The saying that every cloud has a silver lining speaks volumes of truth although it may not feel like it at the time if things are tough. My silver lining from turning blind was that I was blessed with Munch. Even though it's only 18 months on, I find it hard to remember what life was like without him. I realized that carrying on in silence about my sight loss was a very lonely place. Without functional sight, I could quite easily have gone into the negatives of life if I'd allowed myself to, but I knew from a young age that life was far too precious to waste on this soul-destroying way of seeing the world. To preserve the purity of life, you first must allow yourself to live.

Munch was not only the solution to the practical help that I needed (and the most blissful, furry soul mate ever): his job on this Earth goes far beyond this. His calming presence gives people the chance to step out of their busy lives and take a moment just to appreciate the simple things in life. Not only does he give welcome pet therapy to the clients we see in work, but he also does the same to strangers we come across daily. Most know that you're not meant to touch a working guide dog as it distracts them from what they're doing, but it's Munch who usually does the distracting. Questions about him fire at us and people seem to have this magnetic draw to him. Being sought out to dive in for a much-needed stroke has reinforced his reward-seeking behaviour. As soon as he hears the beginning of a question forming on a person's lips that's directed at him, he will head towards their hand, which is at his head height, and wait for attention.

It's so important not to distract a working guide dog, because a loss in their concentration could mean they miss obstacles that could lead their owners into danger. It's important to always first ask a guide-dog owner if you can touch their dog. Munch has used this to his advantage. Knowing when the seal of silence has been broken, he will go to the enquirer to give him or her some much-needed unconditional love that you can only usually get from an animal. He really doesn't care about your appearance, how much you earn, your mistakes in life or your political views. He just cares about you.

Life before and after Munch has changed a great deal in many respects, but it has also remained the same in other ways. My sight may have decreased slightly but overall, life is just the same. Minus the picking up of poo, getting out and about resembles my life many years ago when I was carefree. As a child I'd love being out exploring places with my other senses and making room in my memory bank for these new experiences. As my sight loss has been gradual, I did not notice that I was becoming more adventurous than in my younger years. Unless there's a sudden change in health, we gradually adapt to new ways of life without even realising it, despite the diagnosis.

Post-diagnosis life doesn't change from pre-diagnosis life, either, if it's 'normal' in your family to live with a health condition or a disability. The odd ones out in the family are those who have perfect health, as it seems so different. We have in-house jokes about having Marfan syndrome, as a sense of humour seems to be an innate morale boost when things get tough. Living with such a diagnosis has always made me see the power in the smallest of things that others may take no notice of. It has also pushed me to embrace opportunities in life and the justice of fairness for all has always been a core belief of mine, even from a young age. Excluding individuals with a disability or a health condition is something that I'd never stand for – which has brought about some interesting challenges.

Perception is such a powerful tool that we can utilize or misuse. Even if to the outside world we look like we have a multitude of disabilities and health issues, we do not have to feel anything but perfect. My four children inspire me in so many ways: my eldest daughter Rasheena's uniquely quirky, fun-loving soul; my younger daughter Korisha's drive, determination and compassion; my son Zaidley's chilled outlook, and how he never gets drawn into negativity. Then there's his brother, Jaidan, whose perspective on life I really wish I could bottle and share with the world.

At the age of three, he received a Statement of Educational Needs due to a multitude of issues. Having a statement at such a young age speaks volumes about how severe his needs were. Not only was he diagnosed with Marfan syndrome, which affected him in a variety of ways, but he also had moderate autism, which led to so many problems in everyday living. Alongside this he had recurring respiratory issues, which led to over 25 hospital admissions in the first seven years of his life. Life was never easy for him, but he never once moaned. He is now 16 and has only been in mainstream education for two years, yet has excelled in his GCSEs and is ready to start his A-levels. He does not like labels and realizes that he is more than any medical exam can tell him. The best thing of all is that he has been able to make peace with all the challenges he has been through. He knows that he has far more ability than disability.

There are some things we will never be able to 'cure' in a physical sense, but this should not scare us. In every situation there's always hope. The concept of healing originates from the premise that there's some deficiency – as you never heal from a place of perfection. Focusing on what is 'wrong' with us gives so much power to something that already has us under its spell – if we let it. Thinking bigger than a problem we may have helps us to take back ownership and control of our lives. Changing the statement 'I suffer from' to 'I successfully live with' is enough to begin to get our minds on track to live our lives as fully as possible.

If you lined up 10 people with the same disability or health condition and asked them to explain how their health affected them, you would receive a different answer from each person. If you asked them to rate their pain, all answers would differ, from mild pain to severe pain. If you asked these same people to tell you about themselves, the responses would vary greatly: they wouldn't share a common thread. Ask these same people what positives have come about from their adverse health and many may struggle to give you an answer – whereas others may keep talking for hours.

Consider:

- If you were asked about your health and to describe your relationship with it, what would you say? Do you notice it? Do you take good care of it? Do you ignore it? Do you pamper it when it needs time out to recover from the stresses and struggles in life?

- Has your health always been as it is now? Has it worsened over time, or got better with healing of any sort?

- What is your relationship to pain? Has it taken over a life that was once perfect and pain-free?

- What works to get rid of your pain, if anything works at all? Do you fear that pain will always be part of your life and pain-free living can only be a distant memory?

- If you could name your pain, what would it be called?

- Have you become the pain that has intruded on your life for a long time? Would you miss your pain if it went away forever?

- Do you know who you really are? Without saying your name, age, gender, where you live, your sexuality, your culture, relationship status or job title, what would you say about you? How would you identify yourself and explain how you're uniquely different from everyone else? What would you say that you're not?

⦿ When did you last think about the positives of your health and have a negativity-free thinking zone in relation to your wellbeing? Was the last thing you said about your health or thought about your health empowering or debilitating?

⦿ What health hurdles have you put in your own way by not treating your body as well as you could?

⦿ What advice could you give others about their health based on your own experiences?

Disability and health, therefore, are not as straightforward as they might seem. We all have a different relationship with what we see as health and ability, and there's no standard definition of what makes us healthy. A healthy mind in a not-so-healthy body can enhance life and give it purpose. Weakness in one person can become a driving force in another, steering them successfully through life. Inspirational people throughout history inspire us because they have lived their lives fully in adverse and challenging circumstances. Ability in disability comes from realizing that life is bigger than the things that you may not be able to do on a physical or mental level.

All the people I know with visual impairments are open about their condition and have never really kept it hidden. I connect with their feeling of focusing on the beauty of living in a sort of altered state of consciousness when the rest of society sometimes focuses on something completely different. I really love this connection that has been brought about by our ability in our disability.

Had I been born with fully functioning vision I may not have recognized a voice from 22 years ago just from them saying 'Hi'. With fully functioning vision, my muscle memory may have been weaker (when I play visually impaired bowls, my muscle memory tells me if I've rolled the bowl far enough to get to the jack). Had I been able to find my clothes with my eyes, I wouldn't have learned to find them with my fingertips. These examples are no better or worse than the next person's way of doing things; they're just different.

Ability can only be measured by perception, so should disability not be measured in the same way? The only perception that really matters is the perception of the individual in question. I've never really identified myself as disabled, yet I respect others who do. Empowering people to embrace their differences celebrates who they are and always makes me happy. I love that disability and adverse health are normalized where once they were ignored. Having individuals with disabilities in mainstream media today should have happened decades ago, so that people wouldn't have been targeted with hurtful comments and alienated. The important thing is, though, that these changes are happening now for the greater good of all.

Had I not been born with Marfan syndrome I wouldn't be writing this today. The feeling of separation from others drove me into working in psychological services for the last two decades: how people think and act has always been a source of intrigue for my observant mind, and merging my feeling of blissful isolation with the normality of society has always given me plenty to think about.

Writing has also become a substitute for reading the books that I can no longer see. Entering the world of the written word is still accessible, though, through reading e-books on a Kindle magnified so that there are only eight words per page on a black background. Audiobooks take me to places where the imagination loves to roam. I probably wouldn't have sought out these alternative book formats had I not lost more vision. Searching for books that celebrate the beauty in difference in health and disability was one of many reasons I wrote this book. Finding a book that I could say, 'Yes, that's exactly how I feel,' in relation to the positives of living in perceived incurable adversity is music to my ears – but this type of book was not as prevalent as the more emotional books on the subject. If you can't find the book that you're looking for, write it.

Life is not a whole static picture but a multitude of smaller snippets of reality that we piece together to make a whole picture that changes over time. It's the nature of being human that allows us to transition in and out of different stages with or without drama. Getting attached to one way of being, thinking and feeling can cause issues to arise when faced with change. Getting stuck in limited thinking in relation to how you perceive health can leave you unprepared if things ever do change for the worse.

Whether your pen hovers above a designated box, passes it by or marks it to show that you belong to a box that many have ticked before you, remember to take a moment to stop and celebrate your life both in and outside of this box. Living outside a label can take on many forms. A box can't trap a free spirit into thinking that this is all life can give them. Living inside the box for many may, however, be a comfortable place where certainty lies. It's our choice to live inside or outside the box. If you choose to live freely outside the box, then you may need to find something or someone to keep you company in a world full of possibilities.

CHAPTER 8

Finding Your Own Odd Sock

If a census were taken to account for all the odd socks in the world, I wonder just how many there would be. From the ones stuffed down the side of the sofa through to those that accidentally end up in landfill, miles away from their lonely matching partner, there must be loads. Does anyone else keep a colossal bag of odd socks just waiting to be reunited, or is it just me?

You can tell a lot about a person from the socks they wear. Of course, there are the flip-flop people who don't own any (the free-spirited in the world of foot coverings), but if we're looking just at sock-wearers, I do believe we belong to tribes.

First, we have the straight-laced, black-sock type who never deviate from the safety of the classic sock, neatly paired in the drawers of their immaculate bedrooms. Then there are those who prefer socks embroidered with little logos or the days of the week. These people may take a risk in life if they're feeling adventurous and may even rebelliously wear their socks on the wrong days if they fancy a little thrill. In complete contrast are the 'whiter-than-white' crowd. You can usually find these socks on feet that never keep still, as they tend to be doing some sort of sporting activity. Washing machines across the land scream in protest when heaps of these muddied socks go in. Then we have the always-cold tribe, or those who prefer comfort over style – they go for the fluffiest socks around and will most likely marry them with the snuggest pair of slippers (which they'll resent taking off if they have to pop out). Then, there's the diamond-pattern devotees who fall into two categories: the more relaxed, sporty type who love a bit of golf, and people of the older generation who appreciate a good pattern when they see one. The people-pleasers wear their Christmas socks from Auntie Matilda and complete their outfits with a hand-knitted jumper from Grandma Florence. These people are 'keepers' and you know they will always cherish what you buy them. Those who buy comedy socks and tuck their trouser hems into them, wearing them with pride, are the ones you really need to invite to your next party. These jokers will keep the crowd amused for hours.

The final category of sock-wearers are the odd-sock souls who really don't give a damn about what others think about them. I really like this lot.

My children belong to a mixture of these types of people. My elder daughter, Rasheena, belongs to the odd-sock gang. As life is far too short to spend time searching for a lost sock, any two will do. Her sister, Korisha, must have matching black socks – if a shoe shop calls out to her soul, it really matters to her that she has normal, matching socks to slip into a lovely pair of shoes. Jaidan fluctuates between two groups: in school he usually wears black, but at home likes to mix it up a bit with a splash of colour or print just to feel a little freer. My younger son, Zaidley, however, made an enemy of my washing machine years ago by only wanting to wear white socks. Not the best choice, as he is the biggest sports-mad mud magnet ever. Then there's me: I usually rummage around for whatever is left over. My feet aren't fussy.

Personally, I am rather partial to a bit of odd-sock wearing. as it's nice to have my foot in two camps. It also gives me a slight feeling of rebellion, celebrating the fact that deep down, I really don't want to fit in with what society expects. To be fair, I can't see my feet when I look down, so I forget that other people can. The whole idea that I need to look perfect to the outside world never really crosses my mind. I mean, I've never owned make-up, let alone worn it, as I wouldn't be able to see it and I forget that others can. I don't wear heels as I am clumsy enough bare-footed, so wearing something to make myself falsely taller than I am seems a little pointless to me. Not wearing heels also prevents me from damaging even more body parts. Trying to be something that I am not has never appealed to me, so wearing odd socks is my expression of perfection in imperfection.

As I've mentioned before, when I met Munch I knew that he was also a little different, and if he wore socks he would be one of my lot. Looking and acting different from the 'typical' guide dog, he goes through life in his own unique bubble. He is the dog who splashes around and causes a tsunami while the other paddling dogs run for cover. If we're out walking with other dogs, he'll be the one running round us all in circles and getting stuck in hedges while the other dogs pretend he does not exist. He is the dog who whimpers for an age after Angus the cat kills anything from a spider to a mouse and brings it in to show us. Death really gets to this sensitive soul. He is also not the best at following instructions when off-duty, so he can always be found doing his own thing at his own pace. Why would he want to be anything else apart from himself?

As most pet owners would agree, their dogs are more than just a dog. They become part of the family and an extension of themselves. This is even more true when you have a guide dog, who becomes such a valuable rock in your once-unsteady world. A guide dog becomes a bridge between the sighted world and the blind, insightful world – a bridge you once stood upon alone and unsure. With a guide dog walking on your left-hand side like a bodyguard, it's clear for the sighted to see that you need help getting around places that most go to without thinking. These dogs symbolize more than just a dog: they become a new way of life.

Healing those who need to be healed in whichever way possible, Munch has many roles. For those who have lost a dog of their own, his sloppy kisses help them to remember the feel of their own furry friend's wet love. He has helped many non-dog lovers overcome their fear of dogs by being his true, gentle-giant persona around them. He has helped many a person without a voice to be themselves, to feel comfortable and relaxed. This may be a side of themselves they're too shy to show the world. As he sits at the feet of those with cognitive impairments, he knows that they're the ones who are the wisest in the world. Nuzzling into an elderly person who has not spoken to anyone for days at a time helps them to know they can never be lonely in a world full of friends. His energy tunes into the frequency of the emitters' desires and he becomes whatever they need at that precise moment.

I think if he'd been an average-looking guide dog he may not have been able to touch so many lives in such a short space of time. As he stands out like a sore thumb, it feels like his being on this Earth has an ulterior motive. I don't believe for one minute that he chose to be a dog in this lifetime without knowing he would change the lives of those around him in the most beautiful of ways.

I also think that it was no coincidence that he was paired with me, his matching odd sock. Feeling like I didn't fit in was never unbearable to me and if I am honest, it always felt like a gift. Throughout life I've always sought out the odd socks in a pristine-looking world. Any odd socks that were slightly worn, full of imperfections, rough around the edges or just simply one of a kind always excited my soft spot. They were the ones I related to, as we would sit outside the box, observing the world going by. You couldn't ask for a nicer bunch of people to be with in a sometimes-hostile world. The universe really knew what it was doing when it matched up Munch and me.

What is so great about the world of odd socks is that things tend to be more flexible here – meltdowns over insignificant things are usually the exception rather than the rule. Not living with overly high expectations means more successes. If nothing is expected and every achievement becomes a bonus, you become a far more contented person.

Stress becomes less as we learn to relax more in the beauty of diversity. When we feel less pressured to belong to a society that expects a uniform appearance, we can enjoy our own individuality, regardless of what others think of us. With a collective relaxed energy spreading across odd-sock land, stress becomes a thing of the past.

Life takes on a whole new meaning when it's not defined by expectation. Within the land of the odd socks, many may have diced with death or been born without a fully functioning body, but that won't enter their minds as they speed through life with passion and drive. With no expectations, they're free to achieve greater things than goals.

Encounters with people and events never happen by chance – the odd socks know that they happen for a reason, season or a lifetime, and nothing else.

Knowing this and believing in it 100 per cent stops us from getting attached to situations that will be over just as soon as they began. Witnessing these without getting drawn in keeps these odd socks from being pulled out of shape.

Accepting other odd socks into the fold is always a positive, never a chore. Both matching pairs and other odd socks are equal and valued in every way possible. Similarities and differences make the world a far more interesting place and they give colour to an otherwise bland world. There's no such feeling as divide if everything is whole around you. So as odd socks go through life, things always seem to fall into place because they never resist difference.

I was blessed to meet Munch to make up a matching pair, but not every odd sock meets their mate in human or animal form. The important thing is that if you feel a little different to those around you, you can begin to search for your own unique way of connecting to the universe that makes you realize that we're all part of something greater than ourselves.

Limited thinking can trap us inside a glass bubble, watching the world go by in clear view yet feeling separated by distorted vision. Inside a glass bubble, there are many emotions, from blissful happiness through to total isolation. Life pre-Munch was a relatively peaceful place to live, as from birth I made up my own rules in life and decided what would, and wouldn't, affect me. By not attaching to dramas or lower vibrational issues, I had time to concentrate on the true meaning of life. Other times, it could feel quite lonely, being disconnected from sharing joyful moments that all could see but I could only imagine. The important thing was, though, that I always knew I had the potential to choose to be free of limiting thoughts – thoughts that can keep many people in bondage to irrelevant things.

The potential for success is not defined by what your body can and can't do. We all know of people in the public eye who have used their health adversities to not only enhance their own lives, but also the lives of many others whom they may never meet. They believe in themselves and do not entertain the thought that success can only arise from optimum circumstances, when everything runs smoothly. Our potential is there from birth, yet it can sometimes take a life-changing experience to believe that our potential is there for a reason. To turn weaknesses into strengths we need to accept that these weaknesses are not given to us by chance; they're there to be transformed into the push that we need to go forwards.

Explaining to someone that they're going through exactly what they're meant to be going through, at exactly the right time in their life, does not always go down too well (and may leave you wondering if they're about to use a voodoo doll on you to inflict some pain)! Others will get what you mean and agree with you whole-heartedly, as they know that without their experiences of life they wouldn't be the person they are today.

Life is never static and change is inevitable, so fighting change is futile. Changes happen in every area in our life, including health, so to my mind, accepting this is the best way *not* to get attached to how we used to be and what we were once capable of. If you think of it this way, would you still want to be doing the same things you were doing when you were a two-year-old? Okay, life may have seemed much easier back then, but if you stop and think about how frustrating the world seems to a two-year-old, you may change your mind. Not being able to communicate your needs and wishes, being dependent on others for your daily schedule, having your exploration limited and having to eat foods that others choose may soon make you want to go back to your own body of today. Perfect health can only go so far in making you happy, as health is only one part of your life.

How to begin the search for your odd sock

I know it's possible to meet that odd sock who will enhance your life regardless of what is going on in your body or externally. You might find your odd sock in a place you had never thought to look. So, if you're willing, here's where you might begin looking for the missing part of your soul's potential.

Your smile stations

There's a world full of happy experiences out there, which are available to us all. Don't believe that you're the only one without access to this happiness. Do you know that feel-good place inside – like when you're stopped in your tracks, belly-laughing at what's right in front of you? When you're in this place, you forget what made you cry last night. I call this the personal 'smile station' and you need to visit it every day. Your personal smile station may not be the same as everyone else's, but whatever it is, it does the job for you.

Your smile station is probably the best place to look for your odd sock. My smile station is appreciating quirky – give me quirky over standard, any day. When I first met Munch, I loved the way he was so different from a 'standard' guide dog and even his Labradoodle breeding. It was that exact feeling with which I could identify – as I didn't conform to expectations of how a blind person should look, I knew I'd found the exact mirror of myself, which made me ecstatic. Having always loved batgirl in a room full of princesses, quirkiness always makes me smile because I identify with difference. When I meet another odd sock like me, I feel at home with my tribe.

Whatever makes you feel at home with your identity, regardless of disability, health or adversity, is the place you need to be. Is there something that you love but you feel ashamed to admit to it in case you're judged? It's likely that this is the exact thing you need to empower you to stay strong through difficult times. Announcing to people in your life that your odd sock makes you smile may start the conversation you always wanted to have.

Your own archaeological find

Do you recall a 'find' that you felt no one had found before? An object or feeling of connection that you sensed could change your life and the lives of others forever? That feeling of coming home to a place you were previously unaware of but knew had always existed, deep inside? Something that you had been searching for all of your life, yet could not name? Its old newness makes you happy. This is the power of your odd-sock find.

My archaeological find came when I stumbled across the term 'metaphysics' and began studying at the Metaphysics School of Wales the very next day. That morning I'd read a blurry article in *Spirit & Destiny* magazine (I got the main gist of it by piecing together the odd letter I could see from the tiny writing). It described a principle I'd always lived by without knowing it. That afternoon I went for a tarot reading with a friend of mine and mentioned the metaphysics course. He told me he'd just started his first year, studying with Dr Joan Howell, the founder of the school. A phone call later and I was enrolling the next day. From my first lesson with Dr Howell I realized I'd found my tribe, yet I never knew it existed. These people saw the world as I did (except their eyes worked far better) and I knew that I was not as odd as I'd once thought.

If you've always found it hard to find your tribe of people, maybe you've been looking in the wrong places. We're so lucky now: with the Internet, we have the power to communicate at our fingertips. We can find people in similar circumstances in any part of the world, at any time. And when you make that connection, it brings a feeling of 'home'. It opens doors you never knew existed, empowering and enriching your life in new ways. To attract something into your life, you first need to acknowledge what you need.

Your land of hope

Getting through life with a health challenge, disability or any adversity is not easy, but nor does it have to feel like a hopeless battle. It's not others' responsibility to give us hope; it's our responsibility to find hope in the life we already have. Dreaming of achieving something in your lifetime can mean the difference between thriving and languishing. Hope is more than an unobtainable ideal. It's an innate seed that we're all born with, but many forget to water it.

I've never wasted my time and energy hoping to heal physically from a disorder that affects most of my body. Channelling this energy into hope for all the loved ones in my life to be healthy and happy seems a far better use of my time. To me, hope is also knowing that even when things get tough, there are better times ahead, because it's human nature to reach our full potential, regardless of blips.

The land of hope can include or exclude religion. Your land of hope is unique to you and gets you through the hard times as eagerly as it celebrates the good times. Accepting that your health may not be perfect but your outlook in life is can be all you need to remain in the land of hope. Your dreams and aspirations belong to you alone; you're the only one with the life qualifications to follow them.

Life purpose

Some are born knowing their life purpose, while others spend their entire lifetimes looking in the wrong places. Workshops and books can inspire you to find your life purpose, but it's important to put what you learn into practice; being proactive, taking your own lead and trying out different paths. Thank every wrong turn that you take, as mistakes lead you to places that are right on so many different levels.

I knew that my life purpose from a young age was to be of service to others in any way I could. From arranging a charity bring-and-buy sale as a young child with the help of my parents through to training as a counsellor to be there for clients, I always knew that helping others felt right. Munch has that same energy about him and, although he is trained as a guide dog, he helps far more people than me alone: he was put on this Earth to spread his Munch magic. He treats everyone he meets with acceptance and gives them the undivided attention that can be so scarce these days. People he knows look forward to him brightening up their sometimes dismal day when they see him.

Searching for our life purpose can be hampered by the false belief that we're the most important character in our lives. With self-help bookshelves lining labyrinths of bookshops across the world promoting the importance of 'me', it can be so easy to slip into looking for self-gratification while ignoring others in an absent-minded way. Finding your life purpose can come to you in the funniest of ways when you least expect it, and can challenge your core beliefs. Finding your life purpose to accompany you through life will excite you, motivate you and give you abundant energy. You know when you've found it because you forget you're doing it: there's no struggle, only love.

What's in store for you and your odd sock?

After searching for your life purpose in your archaeological find that's situated in your smile station in your personal land of hope, fingers crossed you will be able to start seeing the world in a different light. Taking your adversity and turning it into your blessing becomes possible when you see life from a different viewpoint. Physics tells us that energy can never be destroyed, only transformed. Replacing thoughts of fear with possible solutions can be enough to start you on the path of a more positive outlook on life. We always have the choice to focus on what we want. If you want the world to continue looking bleak with many obstacles, then keep your focus here. If you want to move forwards and see past your adversity, then it's up to you to find solutions.

There's nothing in this world that can't be overcome. It's very unlikely that you're the only person in existence ever to have gone through what you're going through and, given that others have successfully lived through similar situations, there's nothing stopping you from doing the same, too. Positive energy is always more magnetic than negative energy, so when you start thinking and being more positive, regardless of the situations in which you find yourself, you attract like-minded people to keep you company in your new-found happy zone. Surrounding yourself with positive people makes it more likely that you will remain here and be empowered instead of slipping back into negative ways of thinking.

When you remember that life is a gift and not a chore, you're free to focus on living in the moment. If you have the mindset that everything in life is chore that needs to be tackled and not enjoyed, then you're living your life in a state of resistance. Dreading another day in adversity stops you from looking for the doors that will take you into a positive world. It may sound strange to try to turn your suffering into a blessing, but if you don't, it can be like living under a cloud. Stepping into a sunnier spot may take a while, but it will be worth it. Being grateful that you have the feet to walk the route to a better way of life can be the start of a life-changing future, as gratitude for the smallest of things can make the biggest of impacts.

When you realize that you're no longer alone in this world and you have a 'companion' to keep you going, whether it has a heartbeat or not, you're ready to begin embracing life rather than trying to escape it. If your own odd-sock companion appears via a new volunteering role, a writing group or a support group that's just waiting for you to join, it has been found for a reason. When you match your uniqueness with your matching pair, you can no longer ever feel alone in a world that will now see you as a package.

Your adversity should never define how you see yourself and how you feel the world sees you. Physical, mental, social, financial or spiritual adversity can leave you feeling like the world is full of voids instead of an abundance of opportunities. Trying to find your own meaning in life in such a place can seem an impossible task, yet there's always beauty in what you experience at any given time.

It's hard for us to begin to comprehend that any type of beauty lies in what we're experiencing if there are feelings of pain, anger, hopelessness and a cocktail of negative emotions, but it does exist. Looking at the world from a different perspective can help to change weaknesses to strengths and failures to successes. The saying 'beauty lies in the eye of the beholder' is true: if we asked all 7 billion people in the world to express their version of beauty, the varied answers would be mind-blowing.

So, what beauty can you find in your adversity?

CHAPTER 9

Finding Your Own Beauty

'I do not care if your eyebrows are not on trend. I do not care about the spot you think is huge. I do not care if you have mayonnaise from your lunch on your top. I do not care that you have spinach between your teeth. I do not care that you wore the same top to go out for the fifth time in a row. I do not care that you do not have the same body as you did 20 years ago. I do not care that your roots are showing through. I do not care that your appearance is not always perfect.

'I do care that you're healthy. I do care that when you look in the mirror, you like what you see. I do care that you wear clothes to impress yourself, not others. I do care that when you smile, it's

real. I do care that your body is as well as you can make it. I do care that over the years you've grown into the person you've always wanted to be. I do care that you know that your beauty comes from your soul. I do care that the outside world sees you for who you truly are.

'Seeing is not always believing. For me, sight loss has meant insight gains. A person's beauty goes deeper than the body they dwell in. I don't know what society's perfection looks like, as I've never been able to see properly. I can tell you, though, what a perfect person is like.

'A perfect person is loving. A perfect person is kind. A perfect person is empathic. A perfect person is wise. A perfect person is compassionate. A perfect person is altruistic. A perfect person exists within every one of the 7 billion people in this world.

'I care that although life gets tough, you realize that it will not always be like this. I care that you know how much of a positive impact you have on others. I care that you inspire others *to reach their happy zone. I care that you're you. I care that without functional vision, I can still see you. I care that I am not the only one who can see past your face with unkempt eyebrows, a spot on your face and spinach between your teeth. I care that I can see past your mayonnaise-covered, ageing top on your unique, lovable body. I care that I can see your undyed roots as wisdom strands. I care that others do not use their eyes alone to judge.*

'I care, because we all should.'

The above is a blog post I wrote in response the question – asked, for the umpteenth time – 'What can you see?' Telling people that I could not see much felt like a lie. Although I can't see details or anything more than an arm's-length away, I feel I can see plenty: colours, shadows, shapes and blurs, all merged together – minimum input for my eyes, but more than enough information for my brain to interpret the world in which we dwell. I've learned over the years to see people in ways that are just as effective as someone with perfect vision.

I've been so lucky to have gone through life not caring about my appearance or that of others. To me, we all look so similar; we just come in different heights. At school, children dressed in the same uniform made it so hard to distinguish who was whom. I had to wait until a voice spoke, unique footsteps stepped, a laugh bellowed or a name was called to figure out which clone this was, standing in front of me. Teachers were slightly easier to distinguish, as their wardrobes were limited and recycled throughout the weeks, so the colours of their clothes made it easier to recognize them. Looking at myself in the mirror, I couldn't really see the detail reflected back, and how could I not like something I couldn't see?

I was as self-conscious as the next child, but only because 'not to like what I looked like' was learned behaviour. On reflection, I realize that I never really felt this deep down – only on a superficial level. I knew I had the Marfanoid features of a long face, deep-set eyes, a narrow jaw and an overcrowding of teeth that would make any child self-conscious, but this was discovered mainly through touch and not sight. Comparing myself to others, therefore, was a little difficult, as I could not see in detail neither myself nor in anyone else. We were all just blurs.

When people laughed at the way other people dressed, I did not join in. When they threw around hurtful comments about people being ugly, I really wanted to defend those people from those scornful, judging eyes. When the mean children started to bully one of the more vulnerable children in school, it angered me and made me want to befriend the child going through that torture. I could see plenty of the good, the bad and the ugly in life, and there was plenty.

Everyone wanted to be around the good people – those who never had a bad word to say about anyone and treated everyone equally, regardless of their appearance. I've always loved this type of person. As these true Earth angels walk through life, they leave a piece of magic behind them and you can always hear the smile in a person's voice as they speak about them. I've always chosen to be surrounded by these people, as their energy leaves me feeling happy about myself and optimistic about the world.

The bad ones, for me, came in two different categories. The first is for those who are more misunderstood than bad and I've always had a soft spot for them; the ones who don't really fit in with society's expectations, never seek approval and are happy doing their own thing. They may say things that are frowned upon, but they say it from a place of love and are only speaking their truth. Secondly, there are those who choose to do bad things, to hurt others for their own gain. In all fairness, even as a child I could see that these were rarer among us and that usually, people who did bad things had their own reasons for doing so; they had not simply decided to become this type of person.

The ugly were the ones I chose not to be around. Regardless of how perfect everyone thought they were on the outside, their inner ugliness engulfed them. I remember in primary school three 'popular' girls in my class who appeared perfectly sweet in front of people but behind their backs they were horrid. I never took to these girls and made it perfectly clear to them that I was totally okay with being the only one around who was not okay with them. I couldn't physically be around their sly remarks about other children and knew that they made the same comments about me. Soon enough, others came around, in their own time, to see what they were like. I've never understood why people can be so cruel to others. Growing up, this was the only form of ugliness I knew.

Expectations and definitions of beauty are obviously dependent on culture. From the long ear lobes of Kenyan ladies to long neck appreciation in Burma, physical beauty can't be defined by one generic description. What would West African cultures have to say about the Western world's idea of being overweight as less than desirable, whereas they see it as being nothing but true beauty? How can we therefore ever define what beauty truly is?

We're all are aware of the impact of social media on perceptions of perfection and beauty. That is, unless you've been hibernating in a cave, have no access to any type of media, have too much of a fulfilled life to care, or have a form of sensory loss but insight gain. If we reverse that, we – those of us with sight loss – are probably the best to judge beauty: as there's no one definition, we may be able to provide an alternative that goes much deeper than surface appearance. We may not be able to give you an opinion on which eyebrow shape is best – whether pencilled in or au naturel – but we could probably tell you who has the most beautiful soul. We wouldn't be the best to judge which outfit enhances a person's features, but we would have first-class opinions on other characteristics that make them stand out from the crowd. You see, those among us who don't see with the eyes of the masses tend to see the detail in a person that makes their uniqueness the most beautiful thing in existence. Life is not linear nor static, so attempting to match beauty to an ideological stereotype that's both adored and envied by millions is purposeless. As each atom that makes up an individual is beautiful, beauty can't exist only on the surface.

True beauty can exist in the most dismal of situations. It could be argued that it's one of the best places to find the strong beauty within – when you're at rock bottom and you have nothing left to lose, everything that you do have becomes precious. It may be difficult to agree with this, but if you take a moment to think about it, the logic in it becomes believable.

Our egos would lead us to believe that when we're suffering, our lives are void of any positives. The ego loves pity-strokes that keep us in a victim role; and the ego won't entertain the idea of being empowered by the situations in which we find ourselves.

Exercise: The six faces of beauty

The questions on the following pages are designed to help you challenge any misconceptions that your current situation has no beauty in it. Your issue could be physical, psychological or environmental – living conditions, for example – or anything in between.

I know that working with these questions can be a challenge in itself, but you won't be able to feel differently about a situation by thinking the same limiting thoughts that make enjoyment a distant memory. If you fancy telling your ego to pipe down so you can reconnect with the inner beauty in your life, try answering as many of these questions as you can. Do not think too hard about your answers; just write down whatever comes to mind.

The six qualities of external beauty

Imagine you're sitting in one of your favourite places, where you feel happy and relaxed.

Before you is a being from another planet who has no idea what it's like to be human. This being is unique and is very different from a typical human.

This being asks you to spell out the word 'beauty' with the request that you offer a word related to beauty for each of the letters (B E A U T Y). Think of words you've heard other people say about beauty – you may not agree with these descriptors, but you know they're a common reflection of society's perceptions. An example might be Blonde for B, Exotic for E and so on. Choose words that express the outward appearance of beauty. After you've written down your six beauty-related words, take a few moments to think how you feel about your responses.

The six qualities of inner beauty

The otherworldly being is a little puzzled by the meaning of your six words. They have never heard of any of them because they don't exist on their planet. This being only knows about inner qualities, and can only see these qualities as good or bad. They have no words in their language to describe outward appearance.

To help this being understand a little more about how humans perceive the world, repeat the exercise. This time, go through each of the six letters of B E A U T Y and think of words that either describe the characteristics or personality of a human that makes them beautiful. Take as much time as you need, not only to give the word that relates to each letter, but also to give a little explanation of what that means.

Spend the next few minutes giving this being your interpretation of inner beauty, relating it to people in your life and strangers alike.

Exercise: Accepting beauty in life

For this exercise, imagine you've been asked to give a speech explaining what beauty is and what beauty is not. Take time to think what you would talk about in each of these instances. What is your version of both external and inner beauty? Is there something in a person on the outside or inside that you just can't define as beautiful, regardless of how hard you try? Is there something in you on the outside or inside that you just can't define as beautiful, no matter how hard you try? Be honest – this is your personal version of truth and nobody will judge what you say.

Thinking through your beliefs about beauty can help pinpoint what you may need to accept about yourself.

Exercise: What are your challenges?

If you were asked if you saw your life as a challenge, what would you say?

- You have few or no challenges.

- It feels that your whole life is lived around challenges that seem determined to stay with you, no matter how hard you try to remove them.

- It varies. You have some challenges and you work around them as needed.

What are these challenges? Are they related to physical or mental health, or to disability, poverty, external factors or any other barriers you face? Where have these challenges come from? Have they existed from birth?

Write down your responses.

How challenging is your challenge, really?

From the above answers about your challenges in life, try to turn them into positives. Before you say this is impossible, just stop for a moment.

⦿ Let's say that you've had regular headaches over the past couple of months. These are obviously challenging when you're experiencing them, but if you were asked to rate how much of a challenge they really are, what would you say?

⦿ On a scale of 1–10, when you have a headache, how greatly does it affect your life?

⦿ On a scale of 1–10, how much does the fear of having another headache affect your life?

⦿ Breaking the week into the seven days, how many days a week do you suffer from this challenge?

◉ Breaking the day down into 24 hours, how many hours a week do you suffer from this challenge?

Looking at your responses to these questions, does your challenge affect your life as much as you think?

This is in no way saying that what you're experiencing does not affect your life. They're called challenges for a reason (otherwise we would call them rewards). What this exercise does is break them down into numbers, so we can see their impact in simple terms – then hopefully recognize that these challenges are only a small part of our lives and not the whole.

Turning your challenge into a win

◉ If you were asked what success you've had in life, what would you say?

◉ On a scale of 1–10, how much of the time do you successfully live with zero challenges?

◉ On a scale of 1–10, how much of the time does something stop you from living successfully?

◉ Breaking the week into seven days, how many days do you successfully live your life regardless of any challenges?

⊛ Breaking the day down into 24 hours, how many hours of the day are you challenge-free, allowing you to carry on with the life you want to lead?

From your responses, does your challenge affect your life as much as you think?

———————————————

By changing your mindset from 'suffering from' to 'successfully living with', life can seem less of a hurdle and more of a fun obstacle course, full of ups and downs. Nobody is claiming that living with any type of adversity is easy, whether physical, psychological or environmental, but it can be manageable. When we stop identifying solely with our issues and don't allow our adversities to become 'us', the more power we have. Self-empowerment happens when we release voluntary emotional ties to negativity. Instead of introducing ourselves to the world as a sufferer of a disability or whatever else we live with, let us begin to introduce ourselves as multidimensional people with many positive aspects who can offer the world so much. Your adversity is a part of you, but it's never the whole of you.

Finding your own beauty

If I'd been born with 'normal' connective tissue running through my body, I wouldn't have grown up feeling different. I'd have felt like everybody else. The world may have felt like a far more inclusive place for me. With no everyday barriers to contend with, life may have gone smoothly. I may have lived relatively pain-free for the last four decades and only suffered from common irritations; pain may have been more intermittent and rare. And yet, I may not have learned how to cope with pain without any medication, never discovering how visualization and breathing techniques can relieve pain. I may have not realized, from a young age, how important health is. I may have gone through life taking my health for granted and not treating it with the respect it deserves.

Had I been born with 'normal' connective tissue, I may not have realized that my outer body is only a shell for the astonishingly hard-working systems that keep us alive (and I may never have thanked each system, every day, for keeping me alive). With 'normal' connective tissue, I may have had an eye structure that supported the lens in my eye and stopped any subluxation. I may have been able to see the world like everybody else and not live in an alternative reality. I may have thought life was about the information that only my eyes sent me, constructing my view of the world from sensory overload that never took a day off.

Without all this happening due to my faulty connective tissue, I may have lived a totally different life. I may not be sitting here writing this book. I may never have met on-duty Minster and off-duty Munch, which I can't imagine. Exploring the positives regardless of challenges can free your thinking and help you to realize the beauty in your own unique situation. From clouds to silver-lining thinking, to solid-silver partying, changing your thoughts will change your experiences.

Visualization: The stepping stones

Before beginning this visualization, take a moment to read the text a few times so that you remember the steps. Alternatively, read it aloud and record it, then listen back.

Find a place where you will not be disturbed and get comfortable in a chair or lying down on a bed. It's important to find a place that you feel safe, too, as it helps to relax the mind as well as the body.

Begin by concentrating on your breathing. Breathe in for a count of three, hold for one count, then release for a count of three. Continue this cycle of breathing for 10 repetitions. Notice how the deeper your breath goes, the more relaxed you feel.

Imagine that your chair or bed is made of marshmallows. As you sink more deeply into it, feel the chair or bed supporting your body. It's hard to tell where your body ends and the chair or bed begins.

Now relax each body part in turn, beginning at the top of your head. Tense, then gently relax each part of you, so you physically feel any tension draining from your body, bit by bit. Move down through your body, tensing and relaxing each part as you go until you reach your feet.

Let your busy, everyday thoughts fade into the background and welcome the space that's left for you – there's now a peaceful void in your once-tired mind. This void is a place of opportunity: here, you get to discover the beauty in your life. Spend a moment thanking this void for appearing now, at just the right time.

Imagine you're sitting in one of your favourite places in the world. From a holiday destination to your back garden, in this place you feel safe and supported. Worries become a distant memory and you feel nothing but love for life when you're here, in your spot. All the feelings that run through you are positive and make you realize how lucky you really are. Take a moment to connect with this place and enjoy sitting here alone.

As you sit in this positive place in your life, make a promise to yourself that during your time here you'll only concentrate on the positives. Negative thoughts can be kept for another time.

In front of you, you see a path made from 10 stepping stones that leads to a place that's lit up in the most enticing way; it has an almost magnetic pull. You feel an urge to make your way over to this magical place. As you approach the path, you notice a sign to your left. On the sign are the rules you must follow if you wish to walk this path. The three rules are:

1. On the first step, you'll state the challenge you face. By the last step, you'll get to see this challenge as a positive in your life.

2. As you step onto each stone, you'll think of one positive thing, big or small, that this challenge has brought you.

3. Use positive words on this pathway. NO negative words are allowed.

Accepting these rules, you start on the path and, as you stand on the first step, you say out loud the challenge that life has blessed you with.

On the second stepping stone, you feel a little more confident and say out loud a positive thing this challenge has brought you.

As you slowly step onto the other eight stones along the path, you feel more and more at peace. With each step forwards, you find a positive in what you once thought of as a challenge.

As you reach the final stepping stone, you feel an immense feeling of bliss running though you, as you know that your positive thoughts are changing how you see your life.

Step forwards into the bright, inviting place at the end of the pathway. As you step in, you realize that this is a different version of your life. A version filled with positivity and beauty all around you. Some circumstance in life may be the same as before, but by looking at your life through more positive eyes, your world has become a more beautiful place in which to live. Take a few moments here to look around and appreciate the beautiful things in your life. Take time to appreciate things that you once disliked. Be thankful for the things you once regretted. Just see your life as changed for the better.

Once you feel ready and have taken in all the beauty you now see, begin to make your way back along the stepping-stone path. As you step on each stone, feel happy in the knowledge that you've been able to let go of your old way of seeing challenges.

Make your way back to where you began, to your positive place where you love to spend time, and take a moment to absorb your experience.

When you're ready, become aware of your body, and open your eyes.

Take a notebook and pen, and answer the following questions about this visualization:

1. How did you feel when you first entered your favourite place? What could you feel around you?

2. What was your initial thought when you saw the bright place at the end of the stepping-stone path? What did you think this place was?

3. What did you think about the rules you had to abide by before stepping onto the path? What feelings came up for you?

4. How did it feel to announce your challenge in life on the first stepping stone? Did it feel sad, normal, empowering or anything in between?

5. How did it feel to announce a new 'positive' for each of the steps you took? Were they easy to find, or did you struggle?

6. What did it feel like to arrive on the last stepping stone?

7. When you reached the place at the end of the pathway, what was your initial reaction?

8. Did you discover things here that you had never found before?

9. What beautiful things did you discover about your own challenges here?

10. What have you brought back from this visualization that will help you to look at your own situation in a different, more positive light?

Keep the answers to the above questions as you can use them in Chapter 11 (*see page 231*).

Certain challenges in life will come and go, and we learn to deal with them as they arise. Other challenges may be difficult or impossible to overcome, but we can change our thoughts about those situations. Allowing ourselves the freedom to live seems too good to be true, as our limited thinking would have us believe that life will always be the same. If a situation is less than ideal, we can become a victim of our circumstances. Yet this is not the case; quite the opposite is true.

By following a step-by-step guide, it's possible to change how you feel about a situation if you know how. You have nothing to lose and much to gain by putting the magic back in your life.

CHAPTER 10

Staying AFLOAT

The human brain loves patterns, predictability and positive outcomes – and these three Ps allow us to feel safe in an ever-changing world. Anything that deviates from these can leave a person feeling a little uneasy. When our version of perfect is threatened by any type of imperfection, our brains can have a tantrum. What many people don't realize, though, is that it takes much more energy to choose to have a meltdown than to transcend the difficulties and embrace them.

Imagine you've just been diagnosed with glandular fever. You've been feeling pretty under the weather but didn't know why. The diagnosis answers a few questions but brings up more. Your doctor tells you that the symptoms should go within three weeks or so, but you may feel fatigued for up to six months. At this point you have a choice either to see this as devastating news, or to accept it. Your mind may automatically go into victim mode – 'Poor me, why do I always suffer when nobody else does?' or the 'This, too, will pass' mode, seeing the illness as just a blip in a usually healthy life. Your mind races to the very rare complications that this illness could bring (you imagine your spleen will rupture) or you believe that the symptoms will pass as quickly as they arrived. You spend the next few weeks of your suggested rest being hostile and resentful about having to change your plans, or be thankful for the chance to stop, regroup and give yourself time to rest and dream. Illnesses come and go, but I feel that they all happen for a reason; sometimes we just have to stop.

Ill-health, disability and adversity is a sliding scale and differs greatly from person to person. The effect can depend on personality type – levels of resilience, faith or lack of, support network, overall wellbeing and self-actualizing tendency (the desire to fulfil our potential) to name but a few. When a person has a lifelong condition, life takes on a whole new meaning and their relationship with health is changed. There are certain things, however, that most individuals who successfully live with adversity have in common.

Having worked for many years with people with long-term health conditions and adversities, I've noticed how their outlook on life can be far more positive than those who live without such challenges. From this experience I developed a step-by-step guide to living with challenges, which has helped my clients to turn the concept of suffering into successful living. Making the right choices in a less than desirable situation can turn a person's life around in unbelievable ways.

What follows is the six-step AFLOAT model that has helped to free many clients from faulty thinking around how they allow their circumstances to affect their lives. I began using this technique with clients who had health conditions and disabilities classed by the medical profession as lifelong conditions. This model is designed to help a person transform the negatives of their situation and ultimately see beyond the new label that has been forced upon them.

As time went on, I began using this model with other clients who faced other adversities in life, such as loss, identity issues, financial challenges, past emotional ties, trauma and many other challenges. This model is adaptable to so many different situations where a change of mindset is all that's needed to transcend a challenge; to accept it and then see past it. When we learn to detach from the challenge, we become reattached to the world that awaits our return. Freeing up time that's usually sucked into the negativity of a challenge can allow us to shift our outlook on life. Staying AFLOAT in adversity allows us to be free to live out our life purpose with the energy and passion of a warrior. Staying AFLOAT has never felt so empowering.

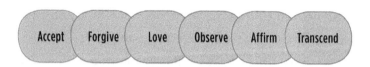

Staying AFLOAT

Accept

Things that happen for a reason can often feel like gate-crashers at a very civilized gathering. Life can be going along smoothly, with loved ones surrounding you as you amble through your well-thought-out life. And then, out of nowhere, you're knocked off your feet by the gust of the phantom gate-crasher. This unwanted invader scatters debris all around and causes some loved ones to make their excuses and leave, while the rare few rush towards you to smother you with help. As the gate-crasher whirls off to cause more destruction in innocent lives, you sit and wonder what you've done to deserve this. Well, this is one way of looking at it; there's, however, a different way.

How about this version: things that happen for a reason can often feel like welcome guests at a very stale, rather than civilized gathering. Life can be going along meaninglessly with loved ones leading you along a very rocky path that you feel you have little or no control over. And then, out of nowhere, you're knocked off your feet by the gust of that very welcome guest. The welcome guest in your life scatters debris all around and causes some loved ones to make their excuses and leave, while the rare few rush towards you and smother you with help. As the welcome guest whirls off to cause more blessings in innocent lives, you sit and wonder what you've done to deserve this.

You see, some things in life are meant to happen, yet we don't always know it at the time.

Many years ago, in one of my previous jobs I was working with a lady who had suffered a heart attack. It had turned her world upside down. Due to the severity of her heart attack she had to give up work, and was left for a while unable to do the smallest of tasks without feeling breathless and suffering severe fatigue. One of the most powerful parts of this story she openly shared with me was that during her heart attack she experienced the most serene near-death experience I'd ever heard.

As she sat and spoke about how beautiful her life had now become, I felt a total peace radiating from her. She was forced to stop leading a life that was draining her and making her ill, and turn her life around to lead a more soul-feeding life. Gratitude, serenity, positivity and hope all fed her soul where once there was emptiness. Later, she used her experience to go on to train as a spiritual healer, life coach and motivational speaker. She chose to use her experience as a trigger to change her life. Her old self would have blamed everyone and everything for her ill-health and been bitter to the world, yet this transformational event had helped her to find new meaning in her once-empty life. She chose to be of service to others. She chose to accept that change happens.

Before I met Munch, I'd always lived life as fully as possible. Or so I thought. Right before I met him, I realized that I'd stopped doing a lot of things that I used to do, such as going out in the dark, as I began to fear getting lost. Meeting Munch meant that I was able to re-enter the world as a different person and show others that life gets a whole lot better when you choose to accept that things happen for a reason. Without meeting Munch, my life would have been limited by my own limited thinking.

To help you accept any challenge you're facing right now, have a think about these questions:

- Do you want your life to disintegrate or thrive?

- Do you want to remain a victim or be a winner at life?

- Do you want to see your challenge as an excuse or a reason for change?

- Do you want to fight your challenge or use it for good?

- Do you think you're the only person in the world going through this challenge, or do you realize that this is a common challenge that many people successfully live with?

A challenge can make or break a person. The only difference between these two outcomes is the mind. Accepting that a challenge has come into your life for a reason is the first step in letting go of the drama, allowing you to begin to write your own story (*see page 227*).

Forgive

Throughout time, we humans have struggled with forgiveness. We have been led to believe that forgiveness involves a lengthy process of stages and steps we must go through if we're even to consider moving on with our lives. Being unable to forgive another person rarely stems from their wrong-doings alone, because forgiveness is bigger than the other person's situation. We all have a different relationship with forgiveness, and this stems from belief systems, faith/religions, ancestral history, personality type, past experiences and a multitude of other aspects. However, these can also be the reasons people give when they're unwilling to forgive. Rather than admit you just don't want to forgive, blaming a person or a thing dents the ego a little less.

Forgiveness is not something that needs to be fought against to protect you from pain; it should be something that helps you to live a pain-free life. Imagine somebody has said something hurtful to you and you feel you can never forgive them. While you're left seething, this person has forgotten what was said and is living his or her life carefree without a second thought – while you're stuck as the only guest at a bitter party. Forgiveness is a gift that you can not only give another person, but it's also the best gift you can give yourself.

Just forgive yourself for doing human things in a human life. That's all there's to do.

Learning to forgive allows us to channel our energy into moving forwards. If we choose to remain forgiveness-free, we waste our energy fighting a battle we will always lose. Some of the unhappiest people I've ever known are those who recoil in horror should the word forgiveness cross their path of blazing fury. They seek revenge on whomever they feel has done them wrong. These people may likely have bodies filled with aches, pains, illnesses and disorders; the onset of these conditions may be linked to their forgiveness issues. It's as if the bitter, twisted thoughts and feelings they have towards the wrong-doer infests the body, which acts as a sponge for negative beliefs. Moving forwards becomes impossible in a body that remains stuck in the past. These people can't progress on their life path because they see imaginary objects barring the way.

We're all different, and the only thing you can ever control or want to control is how you live your life. Forgiving the challenge you're faced with allows you to re-evaluate the important things in life. You're free to use the power of positive thinking to change your relationship to any challenge. You can choose to let it fade into the background and choose to change the foreground into a positive. Both your body and your mind will thank you for shifting your focus from suffering to successful living as you move on with life. When you forgive the situation you find yourself in, it's easier to forgive the world around you, too.

If a problem arises, I am the first to jump-start the quest to resolve it. The benefit is that there's no time for grudges or hostility to develop because things get sorted straight away. I don't struggle with this – if the 'wrong-doings' are undone, then there's nothing left to be negative about. I can't physically sort out the effects that Marfan syndrome has on all of my body systems, but I can sort out my feelings towards it. When an injury happens in my body due to a seemingly small incident, I have a choice to blame or forgive this unpredictable condition for being in my life; and I will always choose forgiveness.

To help you rethink your relationship with forgiveness, consider these questions:

◉ Do you want to live in a bitter or a loving world?

◉ Do you want to waste your energy hating a person who has moved on long ago, or do you want to live your life as freely as they do?

◉ Do you want to use your experiences as negative comparisons, or do you want to use them as a marker of what you want to achieve in the future?

◉ Do you want to use your adversity as a warning story for others, or do you want to use it to inspire?

◉ Do you want to leave this Earth hating more people than you love?

Forgive your health, forgive your life, forgive your mind, forgive others, forgive their behaviour, forgive their actions, forgive their ignorance and forgive everything else in between. This is the only option if you're to see the world in a more positive light. Forgiveness is never a weakness, always a strength.

Love

Describing love as an intense feeling of deep affection does not do the word any justice really, does it? Love is this word that stands alone from all other emotions. Describing it fully could be an endless task, and even then, I don't know if there are any words in creation that can truly express what love really is. It's possible, however, to put into words what the absence of love can mean.

If life is lived without love, it can never truly be lived. Looking for the fear in every situation can only stop you from taking chances that create change. The absence of love means we perceive the world in a way that leaves us free of hope and bound to misery. If ever measured, love is not true love, love is limitless and has no beginning or end; it's an energy that can never be destroyed. You can, however, reject love. Without love, lives fail, people lose themselves, hope is lost and negativity can grow. Love is something that everyone is born with, yet not everyone leaves this Earth plane with love if they choose to lose it along the way.

Seeing the love in every part of your life is a choice. You don't have to hug trees or believe in unicorns to feel the love where others see hate. When you're in that feeling of love, everything around you can only be seen in loving ways.

Our minds will try to fool us into thinking that there are different varieties of love, such as the love we feel for our partners, family, friends or hobbies. But, fundamentally, there's only one form of love and that's pure, unconditional love. You don't need qualifications or training to feel it, but you may need to unlearn lessons that have steered you away from the innate love within you. Choosing to remember that love is rightfully yours is all you need do to bring it into your life.

A lack of love can have a devastating effect, but it's never irreversible. People who come for counselling are seldom the happiest people, as that would defeat the reason for them being in the room. As happiness is a by-product of feeling loved, feeling loved brings happiness into our lives. By helping clients to embrace and finally love the challenges in their lives, I've seen people change from living a life full of turmoil to one full of joy that they want to share with the world.

I once worked with a teenage boy who had never felt loved, even though he came from a seemingly loving home. After spending months working on where this feeling had come from, a revelation came one day that was enough to help him reconnect with the feeling of love that was rightfully his. Ironically, in his full name lay a variant of the word 'love' in another language, yet he hated this as he felt that everyone in the family expected him to live up to his name. As they showered him with love, he withdrew further and further away from them. He'd been born with a congenital heart defect and this was one of the reasons he'd been given this name. As he spent his life focusing on the negative effects of his condition and feeling resentful, he learned to associate his name and condition with nothing but pain and misery. After encouraging him to rethink how he felt about his condition and helping him see the positives that had come from it (there were a few), he began to learn to love himself and the people in his life, which was a major breakthrough.

I can honestly say that I love everything about my life and, regardless of any health hiccups that arise, I know that there's a blessing in each one. Being blind has allowed me to see the world through eyes that not many are blessed to be gifted with. It has made me detach from trivial things; people can get so caught up in trivialities that end up ruling their lives. With perfect vision, I wouldn't have met Munch and wouldn't be writing this book. I love my life with my unique sidekick, and I love everything about living with a condition. Its unpredictability allows me to have no choice but to love change, and to expect the unexpected.

Learning to love your challenges does not have to be an alien concept if you're willing to be human. Take a minute to think about these questions:

⦿ Do you want to choose to fear or love the good and bad that life holds?

⦿ Do you want to see people as loveless or loving beings?

⊚ Do you want to see yourself as an unlovable person, or a person who deserves love?

⊚ Do you want to resist your challenges in life, or embrace it and love it as part of you?

⊚ If you saw your challenges in another person, would you see that person as deficient, or would you love them just as they are?

Learning to love our imperfections is just as important as learning to love our perfections. Challenges we face are there to push us forwards and help us learn to look at our lives from different perspectives at different times. Learn to love where you are at this moment in time and see its perfection.

Observe

When we observe from a distance rather than be drawn into drama, we have more control over how we feel and respond. Imagine a screen showing certain defining moments in your life. As you watch these events unfold, it's up to you how to react. You can sit back and observe, or relive these events as if they were happening now and let your feelings reattach to past events beyond your control. If you choose to be an observer, you remain calm and logical. If you give your power to the drama, you become drained by the emotional turmoil you've willingly allowed in.

When we become deeply engrossed in a situation, we can become oblivious to everything else that's equal to or more important than that situation. If you're unable to change the challenge you're faced with, learning to witness it though positive eyes is the next best thing you can do. We can't appreciate the greater picture of our lives if we're seeing it from our knees. Stepping back and taking time to look from different angles brings us a new perspective.

I am not suggesting that in real life you should sit back and remain emotionless and inactive when situations arise, but I am saying this: conserve your energy for the things that matter. This approach is more beneficial than living in a state of constant hyper-vigilance. Our flight-or-fight response remains active in the brain's amygdala. It has us believe that a perceived threat is enough to draw all of our energy to it, and forget all the unthreatening positives we have in our lives. Acknowledging the threat while opting to step back and keep an eye on it as we carry on regardless is a far healthier approach. If our threat will not physically go, we can choose to minimize its impact by counting the many other blessings we have in our lives.

As I sat in the room of the ophthalmologist listening to him telling me that I'd progressed from partial sight to being registered as blind, I witnessed the words that may have devastated another but did not mean much to me. As I listened to a cardiologist and an obstetrician argue over what was the best course of action to take after finding out the results of a suspected heart attack, I felt grateful that my unborn child and I were fine and we were still both alive, despite my ignoring the warning signs 24 hours previously. I witnessed their disagreement and vowed to get help sooner in the future, yet I knew I was being taken care of. Medical staff came running from all directions. When I felt my eyes roll to the back of my head as I gave birth to my fourth child, my pulse rate plummeting, a sense of calm washed over me. I felt such peace.

Learning to observe our challenges instead of reacting immediately to them can help us to cope better in the long term. Take a minute to think about these questions:

⊛ Do you want to act from panic, or do you want to act from reason?

⊛ Do you want to lose control or maintain control?

⊛ Do you want to give in to fear, or wait to act with power?

⊛ Do you want to rush through life making rash choices, or do you want to contemplate the best choice?

⊛ Do you want to get drawn into the fear-based drama of others around you, or do you want to show others that reasonable thinking creates better outcomes?

Learning to stop and observe creates more of what you want and less of what you don't want. If the things you're faced with in life are here to stay, let them be only a tiny part of your fulfilled life. Be your own motivational coach and learn to observe them from afar.

Affirm

Appreciate that whatever you're going through, you're doing a great job. Living life successfully despite pain or barriers shows us that human nature is more resilient than we can ever truly understand. Saying affirmations helps you to keep your mind focused on the positives when the negatives are trying to suck you in; it can mean the difference between living a happy life or leading a discontented life. Using positive affirmations about your current situation is an investment and you'll reap its rewards. Affirming to yourself and others around you that your life is as good as you can make it gives you the motivation to continue seeking out other positive things, which will change your mindset from struggle to seeing the strength in your situation.

Read through these affirmations and see which ones take you most out of your comfort zone:

⦿ My [challenge that you have] has come to me for a reason for which I will be eternally grateful.

- I choose to see my [challenge] as the best gift I've ever been given.

- As I live successfully, I let go of struggle and replace it with the strength I use to help me get through challenging times.

- A challenge is the best word ever, as I know that I always win every challenge I face.

- I now see challenges as stepping stones to the life I want to lead and embrace them with gratitude each time.

Which one of these triggers the defensive in you, leaving you with a feeling of repulsion? Take that affirmation and repeat it to yourself 10 times in the morning, afternoon and evening for the next seven days. We can only change how we feel about situations in life if we're willing to put the work in and fight through the storm.

People who successfully live with challenges are not just lucky. These people keep their minds set on solutions rather than problems and find ways around obstacles in their path. These 'challenge champions' find mental strength when their physical strength needs to take a rest, as this duo balance each other out. These people are not born with ideal support networks; instead, they choose to rely on their own internal support and attract others along the way, receiving and giving support in equal measure. They fill the gaps in their lives and live life fully.

I feel that my life has been positive, even when negative things happened. As a young child, I saw the world as the most amazing place ever. Growing up, I had positive experiences to reflect upon when things got a little tough. I knew that whatever was happening would pass, as that was how life worked. From the deep knowledge that everything was going to be okay, I learned to love change, as whatever was to come would always be right. I didn't need to go on any pilgrimages, intense workshops or soul-searching retreats to know that with the power of an optimistic mind, any challenge thrown my way could be overcome. I know we all have this ability within us to affirm the positive in life; we just need to be reminded of it sometimes.

To help you affirm the positives in your challenge, take a minute to think about these questions:

⦿ Do you want to affirm that your life is a disaster, or do you want to affirm it as a success?

⦿ Do you want to focus on the bad that has been done to you in life, or do you want to celebrate the good that you've been blessed with?

⦿ Do you want to let the bad keep you down, or do you want to be uplifted by the good?

⦿ Do you want to dwell on negatives, or to use the positives to propel you into the future?

⦿ Do you want to create a pity party with others in your situation, or do you want to help others see the beauty in the challenges they face?

Allow yourself to live the life that you want to live by affirming to the universe that your life is good. We have a choice to dwell in the physical and mental pain of challenges – and this sometimes needs to happen for a sense of release – but never stay in this place if you want to change your life. Choosing to see the positives regardless of the challenge is the way to move forwards.

Transcend

After accepting, forgiving, loving, observing and affirming, there's only one stage left to complete. If you've made it this far and implemented all the previous stages into your life, then it's fair to say the hard work is over: now it's time for the freedom that transcendence brings.

When we let go of the emotional challenges that control us, we begin to transcend into a different realm of consciousness. Expanding beyond our normal way of living gives us a new view on life. When we move beyond what we have always done, we will do things that we don't even know about yet. Transcending the drama in our own lives helps us to connect with people who can teach us the true meaning of life.

The benefits of going beyond what is familiar means we get into an ever-enlightening cycle that invites us to discover the unknown. Expanding our minds and being willing to take on new perspectives allows us to unlearn faulty ways of thinking. We all have the capacity to change: some people choose to do so with passion, whereas others refuse to change because flexibility seems scary. Change can't be forced, but nor should it be denied. We may need a gentle nudge if we're to transcend what we no longer want, but when you're on the way, you'll never want to turn back.

When you go from thinking about 'me' to 'we', you begin to realize that life is so much more than the detail you see. Transcending your challenges is a lifelong learning course, and it brings insights into a world that's just waiting for you. Life can't become meaningless when you give yourself permission to discover how precious it really is.

Transcending into a different realm has always been a favourite past time of mine. Many may see it as living with the fairies, but I like to think of it as a place of solutions. When things get too much, taking the time to step back, meditate and move into a different consciousness is the best medicine I've ever taken.

After another knee dislocation, I corrected it myself and went to the hospital to get it x-rayed to check that it had gone back okay. When I was offered painkillers by the doctor I declined, thanking her and saying that I'd done some visualization techniques and breathing exercises and, as pain was an illusion, I wouldn't need painkillers. The friend with me at the time said that the doctor gave me the strangest look and I had a funny feeling that she was considering a psychiatric assessment for me, but I really didn't care. It worked for me. Transcending pain is not as impossible as it sounds, so give it a go. Transcend, transcend, transcend.

If you want to transcend past your immediate challenge, be ready to embrace the beauty on the other side. Here are a few questions to think about:

◉ Do you want to live your life as it is now, or do you want to bring in some positive change?

◉ Do you want to continue seeing your challenge as a bad thing, or do you want to use it as a reason to find the good in your life that it has brought?

- Do you want to keep your mind closed to life outside of your challenge, or do you want to expand your mind enough to transcend the concept of a challenge?

- Do you want to hear about other people's suffering to help you feel connected, or do you want to feel connected to those who have achieved their goals, despite their challenges?

- Do you want to look back on your life and think, *What if?* or do you want to look back at your life and say, 'I did it'?

When you go beyond the doubt that challenges present, you step into knowledge. Transcending blocks may be one of the hardest things to begin, but when you do, you'll love your new reality.

You choose your own story in life, regardless of challenges, so choose wisely.

CHAPTER 11

Telling Your Own Story

Writing your life story, whether for publication or just for yourself, is a powerful way to acknowledge your uniqueness and beauty. Your story can be told from a multitude of perspectives, depending on how you remember the past and what you want to say now. It's important to choose your narrative before you begin. The questions later in this chapter (*see pages 227–245*) are designed to help you think deeply about your life and your challenges, and to act as a creative stimulus for writing. Your responses may open up new conversations and ideas, helping you to see the value in your life experiences, whatever they may be.

What You See When You Can't See could have been written in very different way. It might be a whole different book – if it wasn't written by me. And that's the point: we all have a unique story to tell and it's up to you how you tell it.

Here's an outline for a book written by a different me. It could have gone like this:

Once upon a time lived a girl born with Marfan syndrome, an incurable condition that would have a horrendous impact on all but a few of her body's systems and organs. As accidents happened and systems failed, she ended up spending a lot of her time in hospital and had numerous operations to allow her to continue living as normal a life as possible. As daily pains stopped her from achieving even her basic goals, she began to give up hope of ever living out her true potential. She could not help others and she could not even help herself. The self-help books she read told her to think of herself and say no to people, as she was the most important thing ever. As she began losing her sight, feeling increasingly isolated each day, she began to see the world as an ugly place; she couldn't see any beauty in her life. She chose depression over joy and anger over peace, and her life became a huge mess that nobody could help her with. As she gave up on the world, the world gave up on her.

Writing the above story made me feel hopeless – what a dismal fictional world. This is the type of story many have lived their entire lives, and may continue to do so unless they decide to change the way they think. I've always had the opposite view of the world, finding it difficult to see any negatives in life. My true version of the story above goes more like this:

'Once upon a time there lived a girl lucky enough to be born with an empowering condition. The name of this condition was Marfan syndrome, and she would soon learn that life with this condition meant that although most of her body's systems and organs were affected, she was given the gift of life. As health hiccups arose and challenges were born, she chose to live an extraordinary life

full of meaning. Living secretly with pains that she blessed, she promised herself she would never take life for granted and felt grateful for each day she lived. She began working with people in need and knew there were others far worse off in the world. Witnessing some people around her getting so absorbed in their own lives and ignoring others around them, she vowed never to read the books that they had read. As time went on and her eyesight failed, she fell more and more into a blissful existence, where the true meaning of life lay. She loved her new life. She chose to see the beauty in difference and peace in hostility. She soon met her furry soul mate, Munch, who would make her life even more magical. As they helped others to see the beauty in difference, they lived a joyous, long life full of adventures.'

When you tell the world your story, be sure to tell the right version if you want to live the right kind of life. So, what's the story you want to tell?

Your own story

Picture the scene: you've been asked to write a book about your life, and to include the following themes and topics to help the reader understand how you see the world. As this is your book there are no right or wrong answers, just your answers. Take pen and paper, and respond as honestly as you can.

1. You've been asked to begin the book by explaining to the reader how you see the world. In this part you can include opinions, beliefs, attitudes, judgements, loves, hates and anything in between. There's no limit as to how much or how little you write – your view might be summed up in a motto, or you may need a few thousand words. This is your space to have your say.

2. Explain what type of life you've led up until now. Has it been a lucky one, or do you feel a curse has been placed on your happiness? Have happy events flowed freely, or have you faced obstacles that you felt were impossible to overcome?

3. Next, think about your health. How has your health impacted your life? Do you feel your health has helped you to get where you've always wanted to be in life, or has it held you back? For now, just give a brief description of your relationship with your health, as you'll go into more detail later.

4. Next, you need to explain the impact of pain. This could be physical, emotional or psychological pain, or any other version of pain that you've experienced. For the reader to understand the depth of your pain you may want to go into detail about your experiences, or just give a brief outline. Remember that your version of pain will be different from another's and that there's no right or wrong way to look at such a complex subject. The important thing is that you have a chance to have your voice heard – a voice that may have been silenced over the years.

5. As we're all born in the same likeness yet into different environments, explain what you think your life opportunities have been since birth. Do you think you've been blessed to be born

into a loving family and support network that's motivated you to reach your full potential? Or do you think that others around you have stripped away opportunities essential to success? Describe how your opportunities in life have made you the person you are today.

6. Why were you put on this Earth? Was it to live your life and uncover things about yourself that you did not know were there, or do you feel like you were born to be of service to others? Perhaps your life has been a mixture of the two; as you've discovered things about yourself, you've also been able to help others along the way.

7. Do you feel that other people are equally as important as you, or do you feel that you have your own life to lead and it's up to others to find their own path? Do you feel that life is sometimes like a competition with only one winner, or do you feel that we need help from one another to get on? Do you believe that success comes from winning, or are you just happy taking part? What does the word 'competition' do to you? Does it

make you motivated to succeed, or does it put fear into you? How competitive are you?

8. Has there been an event or a string of events in your life that have made you change your outlook? Did this help you find the true meaning of life, or a deeper meaning in the life you've always lived? How do you feel about this event? Do you love it or hate it?

9. What do you connect with in the world? Is there one thing or many that give you that 'coming home' feeling? When you connect to this person, object, faith, feeling or practice, how do you feel in your body and mind? Do you sense that a piece of you has been reconnected, making you feel whole? If you had to explain this process to your reader, how would it start and how would it end? Are there things in this world that you can't connect to, no matter how hard you try?

10. How do you define beauty? Does your version of beauty have limits and conditions? Do you feel that beauty lies in the most obscure of places? What was your experience of the first beautiful

thing you remember seeing? Is it easy to find things to match up to this version of beauty, or is it a far-distant memory? Are you blessed to be surrounded by beauty every day in everything you see? Where are the places that beauty does not lie? How easy is it to find beauty in others? How easy is it to find beauty in yourself? (If you worked through the B E A U T Y exercise on page 179, you can refer to your notes here.)

11. How much control do you have over your life? Do you feel that everything seems to be out of your control, or do you feel that you're always able to maintain control in a life that's forever changing? Do you feel like other people's lives are much easier than yours, or do you feel that you're far more blessed than millions of other people? Is control to you an ideal, or a power that you possess? Would you like to change your relationship with control, or would you keep it the same as it is today?

12. When you hear the words 'mental health', what do you think? What do you feel? Do the words scare you or empower you? Do you connect with

others who talk about mental health, or do you feel that you have a different relationship than most with mental health? Do you feel that mental health controls you, or that you're able to control your mental health? Why do you think that mental health is talked about so much these days?

13. What are you thankful for? If you had to write a thank-you letter to things and people you're forever grateful to, what or whom would you thank? Why are you thankful to them, and how have they helped you? Have they motivated you, inspired you to change, been there for you when others weren't? What impact have they had?

14. If you could go back and change things, would you? What would you change? Would you choose to change how you reacted to things, or would you choose to change the things that made you react? What things would you keep and what would you get rid of? If you can't change the past, how would you change your attitude towards past events?

15. How do you want to be remembered? Do you want to be remembered as a person not as lucky as others but who always did their best, regardless of their challenges? Do you want to be known as a person who got lucky breaks, or as someone who, despite what was going on in their life, was always willing to help another person reach a goal they may never have reached alone? Do you want to be remembered as someone who loved life to the max and helped others to do the same? Do you want to be remembered?

These questions have been all about your thoughts, feelings and outlook on life. We do not always consider where all of our beliefs have come from, and so continue to act, think and feel as we have always done – unless we learn to look at things in a different light. As we tell our stories we usually relate the truths we believe, but we do not always explain how we have arrived at those conclusions. While there's no obligation to explain how you live your life, by doing so it's easier for another person to understand where you're coming from. When you relate your experiences, it also helps you to figure out what you've gone through and how it has affected you, giving your mind a chance to catch up.

You've done well to answer all the above questions about yourself, as the whole picture that you've just painted reflects the true you rather than the 'you' that others may judge.

The telling of your challenge

The next step in telling your life story looks at the challenges you've faced. These may be related to health, disability, financial adversity, sexuality, psychological challenges or anything else that has happened. These next questions go a little deeper; they may bring up some emotional turmoil, or they may empower you. Only answer the questions that you feel okay to respond to, and ensure that you have support networks around you (family, friends, organizations, support groups) that will be able to help you if you need it:

1. Think about the challenge(s) you've faced in life. What would you say your challenge has been? Imagine the person reading your story has never

heard of your challenge, so you need to name it and give a brief description or definition.

2. When did this challenge come into your life? If you've faced more than one challenge, give a brief timeline for these. Were they all related? Did they happen as a chain event? Did one challenge feel greater than what most people experience in a lifetime?

3. Before your challenge, what was life like? Do you think you were living life to the max, or that you took life for granted? Did you ever stop to think about life, or did you just live it without much thought? Give three words to describe your life before this challenge came tumbling into your world.

4. As soon as the challenge happened, what changed? Do you remember what happened after this one thing? Were there just bad things, good things or a mixture of the two? Did everything become a blur, or can you remember it clearly in your mind?

5. Use three words to describe life immediately afterwards. Then write down three words to describe how you felt one month later, six months later and one year later. Reflecting on these words, do you now think that things really changed much?

6. What was the worst part of the whole experience? If you had to explain to the reader how you changed as a person because of this, what would you say? Make a list of the negative things that came out of your challenge.

7. Did your challenge give you anything that you had not experienced before? Did it bring new things into your life, whether positive or negative?

8. If you had to give your challenge a nickname, what would it be? Would it be a positive nickname, or a swear word that hasn't been invented yet? Would you want to share this nickname with others, or keep it to yourself?

9. Describe your challenge in visual terms. What does it look like? What colour is it? What shape is it? Does it look like anything you've seen before, or is it a totally new object? Does it remind you of anyone or anything from your past? Does it appeal to you, or repulse you? If you saw it for the first time today, what words would come to mind?

10. How did this challenge make you feel? Did you feel something you had never felt before? Did it just make you reaffirm feelings that you've always had? Did you want to share these feelings with people around you, or did you keep these feelings hidden away from all? Did the feelings change over time and progress into new feelings that became more positive?

11. Share why you think this happened to you and nobody else. Say if you've searched for the 'why' and found no answers, or if you searched for the 'why' and found masses of answers. Why do you think you were the right or wrong person to experience this challenge? Why do you think it happened in your life when it did?

12. How has your life changed since this happened? Have you become a different person, or are you the same person with a different outlook on life? Do you feel you want to go back to the old you, or do you think that a new you has evolved from the experience of the challenge? Do you embrace these new changes now that things have had time to settle down?

13. Looking back, can you say how your reactions affected the challenge? If this challenge happened to you today, how would you react, knowing the effect it had on your life? Are you proud of your reactions and how you've been able to manage them, or not?

14. What did you lose after this challenge happened? Did you lose a minimal amount, or did you feel like you'd lost everything? Have you lost things on such a grand scale before and if so, how did you cope? Was this the first loss you had experienced, ever? How do you feel about the word 'loss' now?

15. What did you gain from your experience? If you were asked to give at least three gains from your challenge, what would you say? Would you find it difficult to see any gains? Would it anger you to be asked about that? Or would you love to share your gains with others to help them with their own challenges?

Challenges come into our lives as a lesson we're either eager to learn or push away with force. If you think of the word 'challenge' it can bring up many emotions, and how you react to these feelings will depend on what type of person you are. You can choose how to react to challenges. By using the AFLOAT model (*see page 195*), it's possible to have a more positive outlook, regardless of what life throws at you. When you let go of the drama a challenge may bring, you make space for a more tranquil life. The challenge loses its power over you and becomes a blessing.

Retraining your thoughts so they become more positive can help you to get through things in life that would previously have stopped you in your tracks. You're more than capable of changing your outlook if you have the desire to do so. Remembering that the world is a far bigger place than your immediate surroundings allows you to expand your mind enough to see that for every problem you have, thousands of people have the answer. Start this new way of thinking by thinking new thoughts.

How you found your own special beauty

1. When the challenge hit, did you lose something in your life you secretly disliked? Were you able to shed an old habit that you knew was destructive? Did you stop wasting your time on things that were really draining your energy and start focusing on the positives?

2. After the event, did new people come into your life? Did they arrive in unexpected ways? Did new pets come into your life who helped you to heal? Did you lose people around you who you secretly wanted to spend less time with? Did the wrong people go and the right people appear? Without having had this challenge in your life, would you have met these people?

3. Did you find yourself in the middle of a chain of events that were triggered by this challenge? What were the good things that came from this? Without this happening, would you still be doing the things you're doing today? Was the challenge just what you needed to begin living life in a more positive way, even if it didn't feel like it at the time?

4. Did you learn something about yourself that you never knew? Did you learn how resilient you really are? Did you learn that you have far more strengths than weaknesses? Did you know that you could have survived something like this without going through it? Did you know you?

5. Did you get to go to new places, both physically and spiritually? Did the challenge help you to get out of the same old routine you'd been trying to escape for years, yet never had the incentive or motivation? Did you find a new way of living that enhanced your life? Did you become more available to the opportunities waiting for you?

6. Did you surprise yourself in any way? Were there things about you that came out to fight when everything seemed hopeless? Did you react in a way that felt like it wasn't you? Is there anything that still shocks you today about how you dealt with the challenge?

7. Did others begin to compliment you and everything about you? Did you feel like people began seeing you for the real you, once hidden from the outside world? Were others more supportive than they had ever been? Did you begin seeing people in another light – a more positive light, perhaps? Did you learn to accept others a little more?

8. Did you learn to value things in your life more? Was your challenge exactly what you needed to let go of things that were doing you a disservice? Was your life turned around by an event that the old you would have ignored? How has this helped you to appreciate things in life today and detach from the things that cause you drama?

9. Have you always lived with a feeling of hope, or did hope become more important after you faced your challenge? Did your hopes change before and after the challenge? What is your relationship with hope, now?

10. Did this challenge push you to change the way you lived? Did life become more meaningful? Did you become more adventurous where once you may have been scared? Did you want to bring others along with you on your new exciting life path?

11. Did you begin looking forwards instead of looking back? Did waking up each morning become more of a gift than a chore? Did you feel blessed to have one more day on this Earth each morning you woke up? Could you start to see the past fade into the background while the present came storming through, leading the way for the future to follow?

12. Did positives start outweighing the negatives in life? Did every cloud have a silver lining? Was it difficult to find the negatives in each situation?

Did people start commenting on how much more of a positive person you had become? Did you begin to feel that everything was going to be okay? That you could trust that everything would happen at the right time?

13. Name three good things that have come out of your challenge. These can be big or small, but they must be positive.

14. If you had to describe how you see beauty in the world now, what would you say? Would it be the same beauty that you once saw, or has it totally changed? Do you now see beauty where you once saw negativity? What words do you now associate with beauty?

15. Share your thoughts about your own beauty. Tell your reader about the beauty you found in places where once you saw misery. Reveal the most bizarre place you found beauty. Give ideas on where they can find their own beauty. What words of encouragement would you give to keep others motivated on their beauty trail?

16. How would you like your story to end? Would you give your story a new title when you've finished it? Would the idea you began with – one of suffering – be able to change to one of beauty? With so many thoughts racing through our heads every day, was it easy to turn once-negative thoughts into positive ones, when you take the time to stop and think about it?

Life will always bring us challenges, otherwise it would be impossible to evolve and grow into who we want to be. We're not here to have our feelings owned by others; we're here to own our own feelings. Just think of it like this: it's impossible to brainwash a waterproof brain. When we seal our minds with the determination to become responsible for our own lives and not let others influence us, then regardless of how hard someone tries to brainwash us with damaging thoughts, those thoughts will not get in. We all have the capacity to live fulfilled lives, but we must first show that we want this. Choosing to see the positives becomes so much easier than living a life full of negatives, because you'll have far more energy for the smiles waiting to become a permanent fixture on your lips. Acknowledging and feeling negative thoughts is essential, but we should never stay in negativity if we want to move forwards and live the life we really want.

Ensure that your life is full of the beauty you deserve, regardless of the circumstances. Make sure your chapters end on a happy note, regardless of the content they hold. Let your final chapter be the one you'll always be proud of and let it be the lead into your next book. Write the books in which you control the endings. Use the passion you've discovered in your own unique life and share the beauty you see with others.

Your beauty is so you.

Acknowledgements

Writing this book wouldn't have been possible without so many who I'm blessed to share my life with. There would be no book without my adorable and quirky hairy soul mate, Munch. Thank you for your unique self which brings joy to so many people. Huge thanks to Lincoln Minster Prep School for sponsoring on-duty Minster and off-duty Munch. Thanks to Guide Dogs for working so hard in helping people with sight loss to lead the life that wouldn't be possible without these magical beings.

To my beautiful children Rasheena, Korisha, Jaidan and Zaidley who have always been perfectly themselves and always inspire me. To my scrumptious granddaughter, Arna-Rae, who always makes my heart smile – never lose your uniqueness. To my lovingly supportive parents, Jennifer and Peter

Cooper, thank you for always being there. Anthony, Calvin and Rhydian Cooper, thanks for being such great brothers. Julie Rees, Erin and Finn, thanks for bringing so much joy into our family.

To everyone at Hay House UK, thank you so much for bringing this book to life. Michelle Pilley, Julie Oughton, Elaine O'Neill and the numerous other staff members who work so hard, I am deeply grateful to you.

To Dr David. R, Hamilton, thank you from the bottom of my heart for reading this book and speaking such kind words. Your passion for your amazing work is contagious and has inspired me deeply to fall in love with my own work just as much.

To Liz Dean, thank you so much for being the most patient and wise editor. You're a star.

Lastly, thanks to the beauty of Marfan syndrome and sight loss that has allowed me to find the true beauty in life.

ABOUT THE AUTHOR

Steven Hill Photography

Zena Cooper studied Psychology and Counselling as a Humanities degree at and later went on to study Developmental and Therapeutic Play at Swansea University. She qualified as an Integrative Counsellor through Glamorgan University. She also studied Metaphysics at the School of Metaphysics Wales.

Zena has been a Schools Counsellor since 2012 and runs her own small private practice of counselling and metaphysical counselling. She is also a Reiki and Omni Healing Practitioner and has run children's meditation classes. She has worked in the field of mental health for almost 25 years in varying roles, and specializes in children and young people.

She is a founding member of The Warriors of Peace Network Cardiff which holds inspirational speaking events.

HAY HOUSE

Look within

Join the conversation about latest products, events, exclusive offers and more.

f   Hay House UK

🐦   @HayHouseUK

📷   @hayhouseuk

💗   healyourlife.com

We'd love to hear from you!